Praise for *Oy Vey! Isn't a Strategy*

"A spoonful of sugar helps the medicine go down, and that's never been more true than in *Oy Vey! Isn't a Strategy*. This book will help you get what you want from work and life, and Deborah Grayson Riegel's stories and sense of humor make the read not only useful but tremendously enjoyable as well."

Peter Bregman, author of *18 Minutes: Find Your Focus, Master Distraction, and Get the Right Things Done*

"Deborah Grayson Riegel's book *Oy Vey! Isn't a Strategy* is a witty, fresh, and insightful collection of wisdom. The easy reading allows the teachings to enter one's heart by circumventing our defense mechanisms. Deborah is a master at being uplifting and enriching without being preachy. *Oy Vey!* will definitely enhance life."

Rabbi Shmuley Boteach, author of *Kosher Jesus, 10 Conversations You Need to Have With Yourself,* and *The Kosher Sutra*

"Deborah has created a practical work that is infused with humor, lightness, and directly useful ideas to support navigating in today's busy world. From more deeply accessing our individual gifts and paying more defined attention to others, to getting things done more effectively with enhanced perspectives, her wit and charming use of language bring this book to life. Deborah's stories are a delight and serve to anchor the principles she outlines. Not only a practical book with excellent exercises throughout, it is a fun read!"

Pamela Richarde, MA, MCC, Chief Coaching Advocate, Coaching Out of the Box, Past President, International Coach Federation

"What happens when you combine years of coaching experience with psychological insights, stand-up comedy, and Torah wisdom? Don't ask! Just read *Oy Vey! Isn't a Strategy*, Deborah Grayson Riegel's wonderfully practical book about what it takes to be successful at work and at life."

Ron Ashkenas, Senior Partner, Schaffer Consulting; and author of *Simply Effective: How to Cut Through Complexity in Your Organization and Get Things Done*

"Clever, relatable, insightful, funny—this book is a keeper you'll read over and over again."

Laura Berman Fortgang, Author of *Living Your Best Life* and *The Prosperity Plan*

"A fabulous collection of heartfelt, authentic, and very personal stories woven into a tapestry of deep learning and practical application. The pefect read for anyone who needs a coach (or who is a coach) and wants to develop themselves or their organizations— and have fun at the same time!"

Garry Schleifer, PCC, CMC, Publisher of *Choice: The Magazine of Professional Coaching*, www.choice-online.com

"Oh, wow for *Oy Vey!* Deborah offers readers a beneficial and some-times sobering look in the mirror—like a fire hydrant filled with chocolate—to help us get rid of self-imposed barriers to extraordi-nary success. And she does it with humor, sass, and vivid stories! A great read that could change how you work forever."

Lisa Haneberg, blogger and author of *High Impact Middle Management*

"A delightful book to help manage those 'oy vey' moments in work and life, lighthearted in style but serious in content. This book is a welcome chance to press the 'pause button' on our daily hassles. Deborah Grayson Riegel's book shares professional and personal strategies to help navigate the personal and interpersonal landmines that we all face, and which stand in the way of effectiveness inside and outside of the workplace."

Hillary Anger Elfenbein, Professor of Organizational Behavior, Washington University, St. Louis

"*Oy Vey! Isn't a Strategy* is a delightful and accessible read. A blend of common sense, careful quotations, fresh insight, and interactive exercises, this book will make readers think about their personal lives, relationships, and professional challenges. Doing the exercises that occur frequently throughout the book helps to internalize insights, apply them, and reshape your daily living. Riegel's expertise as a life coach and her love of Judaism are evident on every page."

David Teutsch, Ph.D. , Wiener Professor of Contemporary Jewish Civilization and director of the Center for Jewish Ethics at the Reconstructionist Rabbinical College; author of *A Guide to Jewish Practice: Everyday Living*, winner of the 2012 National Jewish Book Award for Contemporary Life and Practice

"Wisdom doesn't have to be pompous or preachy. In fact, true wisdom is like an M&M®—smooth, sweet, and satisfying. Deborah Grayson Riegel is wise (and smart), funny (and insightful). She opens life's possibilities while making us smile at the same time. You will emerge from this book a better person!"

Rabbi Bradley Shavit Artson, Vice President, Abner and Roslyn Goldstine Dean's Chair, American Jewish University, Ziegler School of Rabbinic Studies, Los Angeles

"A spiritual guide and life coach all within the pages of a book. This volume is simultaneously witty and profound, provoking, and directive. It is the equivalent of the Sinai desert experience but specifically designed to meet the challenges of everyday living."

Dr. Kerry M. Olitzky, Executive Director, Jewish Outreach Institute, New York; author of *Life's Daily Blessings: Inspiring Relections on Gratitude* and *Joy for Every Day, Based on Jewish Wisdom*

"Combining wisdom from the worlds of business and Torah, along with her own wonderful stories and the tools to put it all into practice, this book embodies the rabbinic teaching that doing is even more fundamental than learning. We need them both, but especially when the latter helps with the former, as this book surely does."

Rabbi Brad Hirschfield, President, CLAL—The National Jewish Center for Learning and Leadership

Praise for **Deborah Grayson Riegel**

"I was absolutely fascinated and inspired by attending Deb's presentation skills training—it was always exciting and encouraging. Now I am confident that I can completely grasp my audience's attention and impress them within the first five minutes of my presentation thanks to Deb's lessons."

Mercedes Benz, Beijing, China

"Deb had the energy and skill to ignite creativity, fun, humor, and strategic thinking for a group of 40 partners at 3:00 p.m. on the last day of a multi-day meeting. Where you would normally see yawns and clock watching, Deb brought excitement and meaning throughout her discussion on motivating employees. Her examples were fresh, her points were crisp, and her handouts were complete. Walking out of the session, I had colleagues telling me that what they learned in that hour would help their future careers and personal lives."

American Express, New York, NY

"When passion, energy, and knowledge are aligned in a training environment, you know you are in for some good learning. Deborah Grayson Riegel is not your average trainer, facilitator, or educator. I quickly learned to expect the unexpected. She came armed and ready to present with an arsenal of tools: genuine stories, relatable analogies, great sense of humor, energetic activities, and practical resources. What I know for sure is that when our time was up, she left me wanting more! Now that is what separates Good from Great!"

Monster Worldwide, Waltham, MA

"Deborah is a sincerely engaging individual who provides the valuable combination of business strategy and interpersonal skills. I have partnered with Deborah at two organizations, and both times her impact exceeded expectations. The first engagement was as a motivational speaker to an audience of 1,500 employees. The second was as a professional coach. After each assignment, both EVPs engaged her in further projects at their respective organizations. After speaking with Deborah for just a few minutes, it's easy to understand why she's an asset as a business partner."

Discover Financial Services, Riverwoods, IL

"One of the best things about working with Deborah is that she takes the time to study our business and culture and customizes her classes to specifically meet our needs. The result is highly relevant, contextualized training that has an immediate, yet lasting impact on our people in their daily interaction with clients. On top of that, Deborah works overtime to ensure that her classes are not only professional, but lots of fun! She has been, and will continue to be, a valued partner for DraftFCB. It is truly a pleasure to work with her!"

DraftFCB, Chicago, IL

"Deborah is a wonderful coach to work with. Her reflection skills are top-notch to help you truly see where you are in life, and her tools help you elevate yourself to where you want to be."

Bill & Melinda Gates Foundation, Seattle, WA

"Deborah is a highly enthusiastic educator and trainer. If you're a part of her class, you'll be touched the very first minute that Deb starts to present to you, and you'll be totally moved by her passion, her professional knowledge, and her skills. I am sure that Deborah is one of the best in the world."

Sony Ericsson, Beijing, China

"Deborah's ability to read a room and assess a client's coaching needs is incredibly strong. While working together, Deborah made me feel completely empowered. She did not ever make me feel that my current presentation style is wrong—only that with a few gentle reminders and minor changes it would be exponentially better. Her sense of humor coupled with her professionalism made our working sessions something that I truly enjoyed. Her knowledge of various types of business makes her a valuable resource to many industries."

Condé Nast, New York, NY

"Deborah is the most energetic trainer I have ever met. She always has a positive attitude, engaging smile, and a warm voice. Her presentation skills class impressed me very much, and it gave me great confidence in my daily work. Her workshop will help me take my career to the next level!"

Computer Associates, Beijing, China

"Deborah is a very impressive speaker—energetic and confident. She has the gift of attracting people to focus on what she is saying and definitely influences how people communicate with one another. She seems to be able to pour her confidence and endless energy into others, making them feel fearless when they present themselves in public. We all love her!"

IBM, Beijing, China

About the Author

Deborah Grayson Riegel, MSW, PCC, is a certified coach, speaker, and writer who helps people, teams, and organizations get further faster and with more fun through her consulting companies, Elevated Training Inc. and MyJewishCoach.com.

Deborah's clients dramatically improve their presentation, communication, interpersonal, and management skills through her dynamic workshops and one-on-one coaching. Clients include American Express, Discover Financial, IBM, Monster Worldwide, Motorola, Pfizer, Toyota, and the United States Army as well as Jewish Federations, synagogues, agencies, schools, and camps.

Deborah is also the former Director of Education and Training for the Mandel Center for Leadership Excellence at the Jewish Federations of North America, where she designed and developed a full roster of training programs for Jewish professional and volunteer leaders.

Deborah holds a Bachelor's Degree in Psychology from the University of Michigan, a Master's in Social Work from Columbia University, and is a graduate of both Coach U. and the Coaches Training Institute. Her unique, energetic, and results-driven style combines her background and experience in coaching, behavioral and cognitive psychology, adult learning, and improvisational comedy.

Deborah is a contributor to *Choice: The Magazine of Professional Coaching,* and writes a bi-weekly online coaching column for the New York Jewish Week, which reaches over 150,000 readers around the world. Deborah and her husband Michael are the proud parents of twins, Jacob and Sophie.

Oy Vey!
Isn't a Strategy

25 Solutions for Personal
and Professional Success

DEBORAH GRAYSON RIEGEL

Behrman House Inc.
www.behrmanhouse.com

To Michael, Jacob, and Sophie
My life coaches

Copyright © 2012 by Behrman House, Inc.
Springfield, New Jersey 07081
www.behrmanhouse.com

Book and cover design: Hazan & Company
Project editor: Terry S. Kaye
Developmental editor: Beth Lieberman

Library of Congress Cataloging-in-Publication Data
Riegel, Deborah Grayson.
  Oy vey! isn't a strategy : 25 solutions for personal and professional success /
  Deborah Grayson Riegel.
      p. cm.
  Includes bibliographical references.
  ISBN 978-0-87441-661-9
    1. Success. 2. Success in business. 3. Interpersonal relations.
    4. Self-actualization (Psychology) 5. Self-management (Psychology) I. Title.
BF637.S8R447 2012
650.1—dc23   2012003995

Manufactured in the United States of America

CONTENTS

Introduction   xi

Part 1:
Get to Know Yourself

1. A Lesson in Core Values from   3
   a Bunch of Flaming Idiots

2. Am I [Fill in the Blank] Enough?   13

3. From Surviving to Thriving: Seeking   23
   Job Satisfaction without the Guilt

4. Converting from Living a Label   35
   to Living a Life

5. When Leadership Means Following   43

6. There's No Time Like the Present   57
   to Unwrap Your Gifts

Part 2:
Get Along with Others

7. Open Mouth, Insert Foot:
   Let Your Ears Hear What Your Lips Speak   69

8. Let It Rip!   77

9. Two Ears, One Mouth   89

10. What, This Old Thing?   101
    In Praise of Praise

11. Aren't You Leaving Soon?   113

12. Learn from Me, and Teach Me, Too: 123
    How to Be Both Credible and Vulnerable

13. In God We Trust: 135
    All Others...Not So Much

Part 3:
Get Things Done

14. Dropping the Latke:
The Perfectionist's Dilemma   **149**

15. Climbing Life's Mount Sinai   **163**

16. Your Laptop or Your Life!   **175**

17. Take a Sabbath for Your Soul   **183**

18. How to Get a Move On Moving On   **193**

19. Put Your Network to Work   **201**

Part 4:
Get a New Perspective

20. Two Jews, Three Opinions:
Embracing Multiple Perspectives   **223**

21. Beyond Shehecheyanu:
Innovative Firsts that Deserve
to be Observed   **235**

22. Finding the Ah in the Oy   **241**

23. Goose Bumps on Your Soul   **255**

24. Whose Burden Is Bigger?
When Size Shouldn't Matter   **263**

25. Remember to Take a "Mazel Tov Moment"   **275**

Acknowledgments   **282**

Bibliography   **285**

Introduction

On a recent flight back to New York after speaking at a conference in Los Angeles, I hunkered down for the six-hour plane ride. As a frequent flier, I knew exactly what I needed to have with me to make the time fly while I did: a big bottle of water (procured after clearing security, of course); two small, portion-controlled packages of hummus and pretzels for dinner (since my main exercise would be reading); my laptop for work and movies (always family-friendly due to prying eyes in close quarters); my Kindle full of business books; and a stack of entertainment magazines for when the flight attendants announced "please turn off your books" upon takeoff and landing.

Check, check, check, check, and check. As the plane took off, I kicked off my shoes and flipped through the pages of *People* magazine, waiting for the telltale "ding" that it was safe to get up and move about the cabin. But within moments, the plane started to shake—not the kind of subtle vibration associated with the wheels retracting, but a series of heart-pounding lurches and drops that felt like the captain was auditioning for the sequel to *Top Gun*.

What was going on? I didn't know—there was no word from the cockpit—but as I made desperate eye contact with my seatmates, I saw that I wasn't alone in feeling scared and helpless. If this wasn't an "Oy Vey!" moment, I didn't know what was. In those few seconds, I thought about my husband, Michael, and my twins, Jacob and Sophie, who were back home in New York. I thought about my parents. I thought about God as in, "Are You There, God? It's Me, Deborah—and I'd like to make it home, please!" I thought about how people would remember me. And then, I thought about my carry-on bag—and I knew what I needed to do.

Unclenching my fists, I grabbed a backpack strap from under the seat in front of me and pulled the bag onto my lap. With the plane still bucking, I unzipped a small front compartment—my "immediate access" section. I fumbled inside, not for a cherished love note from my husband, nor a beloved family photo, not even for a sheet of prayers. I reached for my emergency pack of M&M's®. If this was going to be my last day on earth (or above the earth as the case may have been), I wasn't going to count calories. I was going to count my many, many blessings—and count on a quick hit of candy-coated chocolate pieces to get me through whatever was coming next.

The plane steadied itself within moments of my ripping open the brown wrapper (Behold! The power of chocolate!). My "Oy Vey!" moment was behind me, and I quickly readjusted to the fact that this day wasn't going to be my last—and I am very hopeful that today or tomorrow won't be either.

For most of us, it doesn't take a literal nosedive for us to experience an "Oy Vey!" moment. It can come when we realize that an old relationship isn't working any longer, or that our schedules seem to be managing us rather than the other way around, or even that we've run out of steam to tackle the next personal or professional goal. But "Oy Vey!" isn't a strategy—it's an indication that an intervention is in order. What kind? Sometimes it's crisp, clear, practical direction we need, as in, "Here's what to do, and here's how to do it." Other times, we crave emotional support to bolster our motivation and confidence, as in, "You're doing great—keep going!" And other times, all we really need is a simple, powerful question to help us tap into our own rich reserves of inner wisdom—questions like,

"What do I want?" "What's working?" and "What do I need in order to move forward?"

This book offers you all three types of solutions to help you get further faster and with more fun in achieving your goals. Part instruction manual (practical direction), part chicken soup (emotional support), and part workbook (self-reflection), *Oy Vey!* offers concrete tips, tools, and techniques to help you discover new ways to understand your own core values and motivations, manage the behaviors that get in the way of your interpersonal relationships, get more done with less stress, and celebrate your successes along the way. You are welcome to read and write in this book from beginning to end—in that order. But if you're like me—putting dessert before dinner—you are invited to use the contents of this book in any sequence that meets your needs. Whether you know exactly what you're looking for—or you let what you're looking for find you—this book is for you to use.

In **Part 1**, you'll "Get to Know Yourself" more intimately and instinctively than you might already. Several years ago, when I was considering whether or not I should launch my training and coaching company, I asked Michael if he thought I could run my own business. I will never forget his response: he looked me directly in the eye and asked, "Have you met you?" It was the vote of confidence I needed—and the positive reinforcement I wanted—to remind me that I had the drive and determination to do this. It was also an important clue that we don't always know ourselves as well as we think we do. This section offers a framework for you to become an expert on yourself, so that you can make decisions that align with your values, develop your unique gifts, and find more satisfaction at work and at home.

In **Part 2**, you will discover new strategies to "Get Along with Others" in your personal and professional lives. When I began working with my client Gail,* we were both informed by her boss that if she couldn't manage her temper, she would be terminated. Through coaching, what she really learned to manage was the boredom that caused her to stir up trouble among her team members—and the warning signs that someone or something was pressing her hot buttons. Whether you need to learn to cool yourself down before you boil over, listen more generously, or instill trust within your team or family, Part 2 is the place for you to start this work.

If you're pressed for time, feel free to skip ahead to **Part 3**, "Get Things Done." In fact, if you're reading this book because it's a good distraction from working on the project that really needs your attention, then I thank you. But I also recommend you read about the connection between procrastination and perfectionism in this section, and break free of the attitudes and behaviors that are slowing you down. On the other hand, if you're like me and "slowing down" is not in your lexicon, then this section will also show you how reducing your speed can make you more productive. Of course, if you're going to make positive changes to your work and life, you need to know whether your roadblocks are barriers of capability, confidence, or something else entirely, so you can pick the right strategy to hurdle over them. Part 3 is where you'll find those tools.

In **Part 4**, I invite you to "Get a New Perspective"...or two...or three. If you're accustomed to celebrating endings, like graduations or retirements, consider honoring beginnings instead. If you feel that you shouldn't complain about your troubles because someone else has it worse, I ask you to stop comparing and show yourself some compassion, no matter the size of your crisis. Do you watch horror movies? Camp in the wilderness? Swim after eating a corned beef on rye? All of those frighten me, and yet, I still make myself do things on a regular basis that scare me. If you need a little shake-up from the perspectives that have been keeping you stuck, then Part 4 will add a new twist to your old thinking.

How do I know that these solutions work? I have coached thousands of people in workshops and one on one over the past two decades—across roles, responsibilities, industries, ages, and genders—and my clients tell me that these strategies have made their personal and professional lives better and easier. In this book, you'll see exactly how I used these tactics with them. And this book is filled with the tools I use regularly to deal with my own life's stresses and strains, as well as get myself in the right frame of mind to take on new ventures and adventures.

And while I'd like to say that the wisdom in this book was created entirely by me from nothingness, I can't (or at least I can't and get away with it). This book is a compilation of the lessons on work and life I've learned, sometimes the hard way, from my favorite authors, coaches, and management experts; from my husband and children, and my extended, blended family; from Judaism; and from every client, team, and organization with whom I've worked.

So, once again, let's assume that today's not your last day on earth (poo, poo, poo). Grab a snack (hummus or chocolate—you choose), pick up this book, and let's get started making your tomorrow less stressful and more successful than you ever imagined possible.

Author's note: In some cases, the clients described in this book are composites. In other cases, names and other identifying information have been changed to protect confidentiality.

PART **1**

Get to Know Yourself

A Lesson in Core Values from a Bunch of Flaming Idiots

IN HIS BOOK, *Creating Magic,* Lee Cockerell, former executive vice president of operations for the Walt Disney World Resort, writes about his father-in-law, an admiral in the US Navy. When Lee asked him when he first knew he was willing to die for his country, he said it was on the day he joined the service. "Lee, you have to decide what you stand for long before an incident happens, so you'll be ready to react appropriately."

Little did I know that when I bought my family of four a set of tickets to a comedy show called *The Flaming Idiots* I would need to know what I stood for. For in between the crackerjack juggling and zany shenanigans, I was confronted with a test of my core values.

The three Flaming Idiots stepped onto the stage of the New Victory Theater in New York City and announced that we, the audience, would play an integral part in the show. Having spent seven years performing with an improvisational comedy troupe in college and in some of New York's top comedy clubs, I knew firsthand how important lively audience participation was to a show's success. At that moment, I committed myself (and, unbeknownst to them, my husband and children) to volunteering in any way possible.

Core Value: Contribution

Within the first five minutes, one member of the trio asked for a child volunteer to come up and stand in the middle of a machete juggling act. He confirmed our inklings about the inherent risks by waving his four-and-a-half-fingered hand at the audience. What else would a Jewish mother do when her child had the chance to become temporarily famous but perhaps permanently earless? Well, *this* Jewish mother raised her hand wildly and was pleased to see that her son, Jacob, joined her in her vigor. But alas, another child was selected. Jacob and I accepted this setback and clapped politely for the raven-haired girl who may or may not have gotten her bangs trimmed during the act.

Core Value: Courtesy

Our next opportunity arose almost immediately. A performer called for an adult volunteer willing to don a protective suit while a flame-thrower sat on his (or her! Please let it be her!) shoulders, juggling fiery batons with the rest of the gang. Both Michael and I raised our hands—well, maybe I gripped his hand while I raised mine—hoping to be picked.

Core Value: Recognition

They picked a buff, bald gentleman in the front row who looked like he ate flaming idiots for lunch. Oh, well. We knew another opportunity would be around the corner, and we would take advantage of it then.

Core Value: Tenacity

During the second act, the Idiots proudly boasted that one member of the troupe held the Guinness Book of World Records title for making the fastest sandwich—with his feet. I heard Sophie and Jacob gasp—a world record holder, right here...

Core Value: Achievement

Michael and I gasped: Foot sandwich?

Core Value: Cleanliness

And then the moment we'd been waiting for came: they needed their final volunteer (Ooh! Ooh!), someone who would be willing to eat (Triple ooh!) the sandwich that this guy was going to make with his feet. Blech, of course, but all four of our hands shot up.

We act both in and out of alignment with our personal core values every day

Then he announced that the sandwich would be bologna and cheese.

With that small but significant addendum, our hands fell to our laps with a collective thud. In that moment, we all silently acknowledged that we were out of the running due to a core value that we simply couldn't, wouldn't mess around with.

Core Value: Commitment

Our family's commitment to keeping kosher—the Jewish dietary laws—was being tested. Had it been a nice chunk of avocado and some sprouts, or even a tuna melt, we could have overlooked the feet. But as soon as the announcement was made that the sandwich included nonkosher meat, the addition of cheese was just adding insult to injury. In the battle of core values, honoring our commitment to kashrut won out over our allegiance to core values like contribution, recognition, and achievement.

Our core values direct us, help us make decisions, and drive us to act. They help us determine what's most important to us and with whom we want to associate personally and professionally, and guide us in understanding why we make the choices that we do. As historian Gertrude Himmelfarb writes in her book *The De-Moralization of Society*, "Values, as we now understand the word, do not have to be virtues: they can be beliefs, opinions, attitudes, feelings, habits, conventions, preferences, prejudices, even idiosyncrasies..." Her generous and pluralistic perspective on values is important to keep in mind, especially for those of us whose core values don't always look and feel virtuous. For example, my coaching client Dana's core value

Our core values are often in conflict with one another

of competition feels right and true to her—and drives her to excel—but she didn't feel too virtuous when she was promoted to a management position over her good friend and colleague, Risa. Nevertheless, Risa's core values of generosity and meritocracy helped her feel, and behave with, genuine happiness for Dana.

According to management consultant Tom Glatt, in his online article "The Importance of Core Values," "Core values are truly important to have, to live, and to reinforce on a daily basis." Using his definition of organizational core values and my interpretation of personal core values, we can think of them as:

- Statements of character

- Reflections of our highest moral priorities

- What we give worth or meaning to

Our personal core values even drive the way we act on and act out our Jewish or religious values. My values of fun, family, and even recognition shine through when I routinely invite other lovely, lively families to share our Shabbat dinners. My husband's personal core values of thrift and even competition are what compel him to drive from the kosher butcher to Trader Joe's to Costco in search of the best deal on kosher meat for the aforementioned weekly dinners.

Nevertheless, it doesn't take a flaming idiot to see that most of us act both in and out of alignment with our personal core values every single day, because these values are often in conflict with one another.

At work, you may value both collaboration and recognition, and find that you tend to credit the team more than you honor your own need to be singled out. This can gain you the trust and appreciation of your colleagues; it can also cost you the credit you want or deserve. At home, perhaps you lean into the value of tradition (we have to have gefilte fish on the holidays—everyone expects it!) more than indulging your value of innovation (what if we tried pickled salmon instead?). If you've ever tried to announce to a room of traditionalists that *this* year we're going to try something different—whether it's salmon or a staff retreat—you know that there can be a high price to pay for bumping up against others' core values without their permission.

Whether I'm coaching someone making a career transition, a corporate team that needs to collaborate more effectively, or a nonprofit organization that wants more buy-in from its staff and volunteers, we start by identifying and articulating which core values are really important, and how these are being honored, or not, in word and deed.

If you're looking to make a change in your work or life, or just feeling curious about why your life feels so blessed right now, take the time to see how your core values have gotten you there—or can get you to where you want to go next.

ACTION PLANNER

Step 1: Get Inside Yourself

Look at the values on the next page, and select the ten or so that resonate most strongly for you. Pick those that feel important to you now—not a wish, a want, or a should. Be willing to tell the truth about what you actually value or love to do with your time. Some of these will come to you easily and quickly; others will require more thought. Be willing to try on some words that feel interesting, intriguing, or challenging. Feel free to add words.

Achievement	Financial gain	Providing
Adventure	Fun	Recognition
Autonomy	Helpfulness	Relating to God
Beauty	Holiness	Relationships
Bliss	Impact	Religion
Building	Improvement	Respect
Cleanliness	Independence	Reward
Collaboration	Influence	Risk
Community	Innovation	Security
Compassion	Inspiration	Service
Connection	Integrity	Sharing
Contribution	Intelligence	Speed
Courtesy	Invention	Support
Creativity	Leading	Teaching
Elegance	Learning	Teamwork
Empathy	Mastery	Tenderness
Encouragement	Observance	Tradition
Excellence	Perfection	Wealth
Experimentation	Planning	Winning
Faithfulness	Pride	
Family	Professionalism	

Step 2: Get Specific

Narrow your list to five by comparing each of your ten values with each of the others and asking yourself, "Which one of these *really* drives me?"

My five core values are:

1. _____   4. _____

2. _____   5. _____

3. _____

Step 3: Get Honest

Now that you have your list of five, think about a time when you acted in alignment with each of those values. How were you behaving? What were you thinking? How did it feel? Be as specific as possible.

Core Value	In alignment: What was the situation?	What was I doing?	What was I thinking?	How did it feel?

Now think about a time when you acted against your core values or were confronted with someone who was "bumping up against" your values. How were you behaving? What were you thinking? How did it feel? Again, be as specific as possible.

Core Value	Out of alignment: What was the situation?	What was I doing?	What was I thinking?	How did it feel?

Finally, reflect on your current situation in work and life. What core values are you actively honoring on a regular basis? Which ones are you ignoring or pushing aside?

Core Value	How is this being honored in my personal life?	How is this being honored in my professional life?

Step 4: Get Busy

For each value that isn't getting the care it deserves, choose one action you can take or decision you will make in the next thirty days to better feed your needs. Write each one down, and create small, manageable steps to get there.

Core Value	If I honor this value more, I will have/feel/be able to...	What decision will I make that will honor this value?	What action will I take that will honor this value?	How will I know when I have done this well?

Step 5: Get Connected

Who can you invite to help you stay accountable to yourself? For each value, pick someone you trust to keep you on your path to core values alignment.

I will ask _____ to help me stay accountable to honoring my core value of _____ because he/she _____ .

I will ask _____ to help me stay accountable to honoring my core value of _____ because he/she _____ .

I will ask _____ to help me stay accountable to honoring my core value of _____ because he/she _____ .

I will ask _____ to help me stay accountable to honoring my core value of _____ because he/she _____ .

I will ask _____ to help me stay accountable to honoring my core value of _____ because he/she _____ .

2

Am I [Fill in the Blank] Enough?

AFTER ONE WEEK of living and working in China, with three more to go, I came upon a lovely sight and felt my heart skip a beat.

It wasn't the Great Wall, one of the Seven Wonders of the World.

It wasn't Tiananmen Square, where blood was shed in the quest for democracy.

It wasn't the Water Cube, where Michael Phelps made Olympic history.

It was the sight of a curly-haired woman searching for the community-led Friday night Kabbalat Shabbat service—the welcoming of the Jewish Sabbath—being held at the Capital Club in Beijing's bustling Chaoyang district. It was another wandering Jew. For the first time since I had flown eight thousand miles from New York, I felt as if I was home.

As I took my seat in the community room and picked up my prayer book, I knew that I wanted to savor every one of the Shabbat melodies that I rush through, or ignore completely, on Friday nights at home. My kids are always hungry, my husband is exhausted, and, frankly, I'm hungry and tired, too. But here, with only my own needs to cater to, I was going to fully enjoy the extended play versions of the traditional Friday night songs, *L'cha Dodi, V'shamru,* and *Yism'chu.* I was going to make sure that God heard my thank-yous for the blessings of getting me to China safely, for watching over my family, and for bringing me to a community of my people so far away from my regular "my people." Oh yes, I was going to sing it, sister.

But as soon as I began to sing, I started to cry.

It was a slow, silent welling of tears I could pretend was the result of a week living in one of the most polluted cities in the world, and perhaps a little postflight postnasal drip. I could fool the fellow sitting next to me. But I wasn't fooling myself.

I was overwhelmed. For a week I had been immersed in a language I couldn't speak, understand, or read. I was living in a culture with social customs that didn't make sense (spitting!) and constructs that made my life challenging (squat toilets!). I was out of my comfort zone. I was functionally and culturally illiterate.

I wasn't crying because of that. Nor was I crying because I missed

Learning to feel more Jewish was like trying to climb the Great Wall

my family and my home, which I certainly did. I was crying because, as the first familiar strains of Shabbat songs left my lips, I realized that I finally felt Jewish enough to be an organic part of a public celebration—less like an imposter, more like a native. And having spent the first twenty years of my life as a functionally and culturally illiterate Jew, this was no laughing matter. As Betty Friedan asked in *The Feminine Mystique:* "How did Chinese women, after having their feet bound for many generations, finally discover they could run?" After having my Jewish education bound for at least a generation, it took a trip halfway around the world for me to realize that I could run with the Jews.

In addition to my work with corporate clients, I also coach and train professionals and volunteers from synagogues and Federations to schools and agencies. Part of my commitment to working with Jewish organizations comes from my interest in helping people gain and grow the skills, confidence, and motivation they need to do mission-driven work that directly impacts the lives of Jews around the world. And part of my commitment to doing this work is about challenging myself to gain and grow the skills, confidence, and motivation I need to keep educating myself Jewishly. I must admit, it doesn't come naturally. Sure, for my work, I know how to do research so that I can learn about and share the leadership traits of Miriam and Moses, cull workplace wisdom from *Pirkei Avot* (a compilation of ethical teachings also known as *The Ethics of the Fathers*), and all that Jewish jazz. It's a personal and professional challenge to keep educating myself on "what's Jewish about today's topic"—and one that I'm more than willing to take on. But I always feel behind. Having been raised without any formal Jewish education, it wasn't until college that I came to learn anything at all about Judaism. After college, I made a commitment to engage more actively in Jewish life, and as a kinesthetic learner, I chose to learn by doing. I did Shabbat, I did the holidays, I did kashrut (keeping kosher), I did…I did…I did.

But just like my first week in China, I felt completely overwhelmed by Judaism. Learning to feel more Jewish was like trying to climb the Great Wall—insurmountable, enormous, endless. I was confronted by Hebrew, a language I couldn't speak, understand, or read. I was living in a culture that had social customs that weren't a part of my upbringing. I recall visiting a friend who was sitting *shiva*, the week-long Jewish mourning ritual, for his mother. He was seated in a low chair, as is the tradition for those in mourning. If my expensive Columbia University Social Work education taught me anything, it was to "be where the client is," so I unwittingly took the low chair right next to him, to connect more closely. I didn't know it was reserved for his sister, the other mourner. I didn't know why I was getting strange, even hostile looks. I didn't know what I didn't know.

At every synagogue service, as I struggled to read the prayers written in what looked to me like an off-price brand of aleph-bet soup, I wondered, "Am I Jewish enough yet?" At every holiday, when my father-in-law reminded us, "So, the tradition is…," I knew that I was the only one at the table who really needed reminding.

For a self-diagnosed know-it-all like me, it has been a daily struggle to live in a Jewish world where I feel like a foreigner. It's all relative, I realize. I know more than my parents know. But I know significantly less than my children, who, by fourth grade at their Solomon Schechter day school, could speak Hebrew like young sabras (native-born Israelis), read Torah like I used to read Judy Blume, and understand everything my husband says to them in Hebrew.

But when I helped my son, Jacob, with his Hebrew reading last month, and corrected him when he misread a word, I realized that my doing was becoming knowing. When I said, "Look again, it's a *reish,* not a *dalet,*" Jacob 's jaw dropped as if I'd just announced that I'd had a second, secret family for years, whom I'd been visiting on all my "business trips." "How did you know that?" he asked, stunned. "Dunno.

I realized I could run with the Jews

Just did. Now read it again." I brushed it off, acting like it was no big deal. It was a huge deal.

So here I was in China. I couldn't summon medical help if I got hurt or yell for the police if I got robbed. Heck, I didn't even know how to order bottled water in a restaurant. But I had made a point of learning to say *"wo bu shiro"* (I'm a vegetarian) at any restaurant, so I could order vegetarian foods, avoiding treif (unkosher foods). I had found out where the Chabad House and the community congregation were, and where the one kosher restaurant was, in case I absolutely, positively had to have some schnitzel. These small acts made me feel Jewish enough on the inside, regardless of how "Jewish enough" I looked or sounded on the outside. As journalist and humanitarian Ruth Gruber wrote, "I realized that even if we were born Jews, there was a moment in our lives when we became Jews." I was having that moment.

And apparently, I had learned enough to sing the songs that people sing to say thank you. Not just any people. *My* people. That Friday night in Beijing, as I sang in Hebrew (and wept), praying to a God

I'm getting to know and feeling like I totally and completely belonged there, I realized that my personal "Great Wall" wasn't too big to climb. Even as I celebrate my monumental achievement and look forward to the miles (and miles and miles and miles) of the journey ahead, I know that I am already Jewish enough.

ACTION PLANNER

How do you recognize the feeling of being or having "enough" in your life? What is present for you? What is absent?

When I feel like I am "enough," I experience the following sensations: (Example: calm, peaceful, generous, excited)

_____

_____

When I feel like I am "enough," I notice the absence of the following: (Example: anxiety, wanting, judgment)

_____

_____

When you think about being Jewish (please insert your own religion or spiritual practice here), what gives you the feeling of "enough"?

I feel "Jewish enough" when I do: _____

I feel "Jewish enough" when I see: _____

I feel "Jewish enough" when I participate in: _____

I feel "Jewish enough" when I connect with: _____

I feel "Jewish enough" when I know: _____

I feel "Jewish enough" when people say to me: _____

I feel "Jewish enough" when _____

_____

_____

What messages do you hear or observations do you make that result in your feeling less than "Jewish enough"? Is there anything useful to you in those messages? If not, how might you silence them?

Messages/Observations From Whom/Where	Is this useful to me? How so?	What part isn't useful?	How might I silence the unhelpful part of this message?
Example: "You're not a good Jew if you don't keep kosher." From fellow day school parents.	Useful: Reminds me that my children might feel pressured and that I need to talk with them about it.	Not useful: I don't like feeling judged.	Remind myself that keeping kosher is a personal decision and that nobody else's decision has to impact mine.

In what other areas of your work and life would conducting an "Enough Audit" (like the one you just completed for "Jewish Enough") be helpful? Check as many as apply.

☐ Work and Career

☐ Finances

☐ Health

☐ Energy

☐ Parenting

☐ Extended Family

☐ Romance/Intimate Partnership

☐ Friendship

☐ Spirituality

☐ Personal Character Development

☐ Life Skills

☐ Time

☐ Stress

For as many as you checked off, take yourself through an "Enough Audit" filling in the blanks below.

When you think about your [career, finances, parenting, etc.], what gives you the feeling of "enough"?

I feel [example: "professionally successful enough"]

_____ when I do:

_____

I feel _____ enough when I see: _____

I feel _____ enough when I participate in:_____

I feel_____ enough when I connect with: _____

I feel _____ enough when I know: _____

19

I feel _____ enough when people say to me:

_____

I feel _____ enough when _____

_____

_____

_____

What messages do you hear or observations do you make that result in your feeling less than "_____ enough"? What is useful to you in those messages? If they are not useful, how might you silence them?

Messages/Observations	From whom/where	How is this useful to me? What part isn't useful?	How might I silence the unhelpful part of this message?
Example: You're not professionally successful if you don't earn a six-figure salary.	My mother.	Useful: It's a good reminder that everyone has different values. Not useful: I don't like feeling that I made a career mistake.	Remind myself that I have a job that I love, which earns me a livable wage, which is more important to me than making a lot of money. Remind myself that I am an adult. I only need to please myself, not my mother, with my career choices.

AM I [FILL IN THE BLANK] ENOUGH?

Messages/Observations	From whom/where	How is this useful to me? What part isn't useful?	How might I silence the unhelpful part of this message?

From Surviving to Thriving:
Seeking Job Satisfaction without the Guilt

WHEN WE THINK of the term "survivor's guilt," we typically think of those people who have emerged relatively unscathed from a tragic accident, those who have lived to rebuild their lives after war, or even the spouse or sibling of someone struck by a fatal illness. Over the past several years, however, a new and growing breed of survivors has emerged, with guilt firmly intact: those who have kept their jobs despite endless rounds of layoffs, closures, and foreclosures.

In my role as a coach, I have supported dozens of professionals in managing the despair they experienced when they were let go from a job they loved. But I have also coached many, many more individuals who were able to hang on to their jobs, while they watched their friends, colleagues, and loved ones turn in their name badges and box up their personal effects. There was pain in leaving and pain in staying, and I quickly learned that it's impossible and fruitless to compare the guilt of remaining to the agony of being let go.

It also became clear that dealing with the grief and guilt of survival is only one part of coping. The next step begins when those who stay are ready to shift their thinking from job survival to job satisfaction. In other words, the real work begins when we are able to replace the question, "Do I have a job?" with this one: "How do I make the job I have more fulfilling?"

The interest in meaningful work is an old one. In the early 1970s, Pulitzer Prize-winning author Studs Terkel told us how people felt about their jobs and why so many of us want more from work. In his book *Working*, which is based on interviews with workers in a wide variety of jobs, Terkel captured their feelings about the daily grind. "Work," he said, "is about daily meaning as well as daily bread. For

The next step is to shift your thinking from job survival to job satisfaction

recognition as well as cash; for astonishment rather than torpor; in short, for a sort of life rather than a Monday through Friday sort of dying... We have a right to ask of work that it include meaning, recognition, astonishment, and life." What's important to keep in mind is that we can exercise that right even when others have lost those rights along with their jobs.

Indeed, finding pleasure in work is a lifelong, ever evolving pursuit. In *The Journey Home* by Joyce Antler, Betty Friedan reports: "When I still used to say prayers, even as a child, after the 'Now I lay me down to sleep' and the Sh'ma Yisrael [the central Jewish prayer said, among other times, before sleep], I would pray for a 'boy to like me best' and a 'work of my own to do' when I grew up." And the pursuit of professional satisfaction is one worth chasing. "Happiness does matter from both an individual viewpoint and in terms of business sustainability," says Jessica Pryce-Jones, author of *Happiness at Work*. From her five-year study of three thousand employees, Pryce-Jones found that when we're happy at work, we are likely to be 180 percent happier with life overall, have 180 percent more energy, and be at least 47 percent more productive than our least happy colleagues.

I learned several critical lessons about this quest from my other job—being a mom. My son, Jacob, is long on wants (LEGOs, comic books, plastic superheroes) and short on cash. He is also short on marketable skills, which is not surprising, since the New York State elementary school curriculum seems to favor imparting academic knowledge over work readiness.

Jacob had been an all-star bread baker for years (getting by with a little help from his parents), and, buoyed by the compliments from gushing dinner guests who thought his challahs were second to none, Jacob decided that this was how he would make his livelihood. Yes, Jacob informally launched "Jacob's 'Kosher Enough' Bakery" to earn himself, well, a little bread. He expanded from plain challahs to baguettes, rye, cinnamon-raisin, and onion bread. With work that didn't require him to change out of his pajamas, and local relatives willing to purchase his products at a rate of four dollars per loaf, this gig seemed to provide Jacob with job satisfaction—for now.

Why "for now"?

The job does not stimulate his intellect. (I think I caught him reading *Harry Potter and the Chamber of Secrets* while he kneaded a challah).

The job does not provide a dependable income. (Some weeks, bread baking had to be sacrificed for homework, sports, or sleep.)

The job requires direct supervision—and the supervisor isn't always available. (He's not old enough to use the oven or the mixer on his own.)

But Jacob wasn't focused on the "nots." He concentrated on the job satisfaction that he was getting:

His job allows him to help people directly. (I'm not just his mother, I'm also a buyer—and I can vouch for this.)

His job pays him a reasonable wage (Four dollars a loaf is good income for a kid, especially when a batch of dough yields four to six loaves at a time.)

His job affords him good work-life balance. (He's closed during school hours, synagogue services, TV time, and basically, whenever he wants.)

Jacob had found a job that met more of his needs than it didn't, and he kept it up until a better job with more income stability and consistent demand—chores around the house—came his way. He still bakes, but now it's more for pleasure than profit. My hope for him as his coach (I mean, mom) is that he will always remember doing work that makes him feel satisfied and want nothing less for himself as he grows up. Of course, finding work that meets our needs and brings us fulfillment isn't child's play. It's core to our adult identities.

In his book *Happiness at Work*, Srikumar Rao contends that we can increase our work satisfaction by identifying as many elements as possible that already make us happy in our jobs and focusing on those. In addition, he suggests that we pick one aspect of our work

Finding pleasure in work is a lifelong, ever-evolving pursuit

that we find fulfilling and undertake a project to further amplify it. The key is consistency: we need to do something every day that brings this element to the forefront of our jobs and our minds. Rao believes that over time, we can craft our jobs into work that makes us feel truly alive.

No matter what motivates us at work, it's critical to our overall job fulfillment to understand what we need and expect from our jobs. Naming what we want helps us see what's missing, but it also allows us to see a glass half-full. We must shift our focus from the parts that are subpar to those that satisfy us.

According to the Mayo Clinic's online article "Job Satisfaction: How to Make Work More Rewarding," there are three different ways that individuals approach work.

1. **It's a job.** With this approach, we are focused on the financial benefits of our jobs. While we may not care deeply about the work itself, we reap the fiscal benefits and use the money to make other parts of our lives satisfying.

2. **It's a career.** With this approach, professional advancement is critical for our satisfaction. We want the status, prestige,

and perhaps even the power that comes with our work. We are committed to our jobs as part of an overall career strategy and are likely to keep our jobs as long as they satisfy our need to move up.

3. **It's a calling.** When our work brings us deep personal and professional satisfaction—when our job feels like our soul mate—it's a calling. While money may be a factor and advancement may be important, neither feels as imperative as a deep sense of connection to the actual work we do and the impact we make.

In my coaching work with employees, as well as with managers who want to retain their staff, I have identified twelve factors of job satisfaction. While none of us need to meet every objective, all of us need meet some of these goals:

1. **Money.** Current-earning and future-earning potential is core to this aspect of job satisfaction. Those of us who are motivated by money find fulfillment when we are paid a competitive wage—or more—for our performance. When a higher-paying job comes along, we tend to move on.

2. **Stability.** For those of us who view our work primarily as a way to provide for ourselves or our families, having a dependable income is critical. In tough economic times, particularly when layoffs are rampant and new jobs are hard to come by, those of us who might not normally regard this element as vital to our happiness may find ourselves moving it higher up the list. Stability can also refer to internal stability within the organization. Some of us prefer to work for organizations in which internal change (of personnel, policies, and procedures) is minimal.

3. **Advancement.** Move up or move out! Some of us find satisfaction in moving up the corporate ladder, either within an organization or within an industry. We want to know that our hard work will be rewarded with a steady progression that affords us more power, status, responsibility, and/or monetary rewards.

4. **Recognition.** Some of us prefer to work under the radar, while others of us want to be seen, heard, and acknowledged for our contributions. Recognition is about being "caught" doing the right thing. Some of us may want private recognition while others prefer public accolades. In either case, if recognition motivates us, we shouldn't keep it a secret.

5. **Impact.** Does your primary joy in going to work stem from the difference you make in the world, in other people, in your field or industry, or in your organization itself? If so, you get satisfaction from contributing, and from understanding how your contribution matters in the big picture.

6. **Flow.** Those of us who are motivated by the very act of doing the work are "in flow." We get satisfaction from the process (perhaps even more than the product) and relish the means to the end as much as the end itself.

7. **Mastery.** If becoming the best at something feels important to you, then mastery may be a key motivator. Many of us derive great satisfaction from learning on the job, steadily increasing our mastery of our skills and abilities, and then becoming so proficient that we teach others.

8. **Autonomy.** Many of us thrive on the power of choice. If you derive pleasure from calling most—if not all—of the shots, then this factor is crucial for you. Whether you like to be in

charge of the schedule, the team, how work gets done, or even what gets done, and you don't have a say in it, you will feel frustrated.

9. **Expression.** You don't have to be an artist to crave creative expression. Those of us who are motivated by sharing our passions, values, and ideas place high value on working in an atmosphere that allows the work we do to reflect who we are.

10. **Physical Environment.** Whether a big-city skyscraper or a yurt at a retreat center, location matters. Many of us derive joy from the actual physical location in which we work, and the perks (like an onsite barista) or simplicity (like a mountain view) can make all the difference to our well-being at work.

11. **Relationships.** Studies show that having at least one close interpersonal relationship at work makes a significant impact on how long we stay at a job. And if one isn't nearly enough for you, this may be your primary source of job satisfaction. Whether it's your clients or your colleagues, you take great pleasure in interacting with others in a meaningful way.

12. **Work-Life Integration.** If you derive significant pleasure from working in an environment in which your professional and personal commitments are appreciated and respected, then this may be especially important for your job satisfaction. You are happiest when your personal life doesn't suffer as a result of your work life, and vice versa, and are most satisfied when your personal and professional personas can integrate seamlessly.

Your personal combination of motivating and satisfying factors will be just that—deeply personal to you. Aviel Barclay, the first *soferet* (female Jewish ritual scribe), told *Moment* magazine, "One of the things that has kept my inspiration for the service of God and the Jewish people has been what Rabbi Jacob Isaac Horowitz, said: 'One cannot tell another which way to follow…. Each one must see to which way he is attracted, and in this way he is to serve with all his strength.' That and the knowledge deep in the core of my soul that I am supposed to do this."

According to Yalkut Shimoni, an anthology of biblical lore, "One should be thankful to a place from which one gains contentment." We are allowed to want more for ourselves from work—passion, self-direction, and even pleasure. No job offers it all. No job could. While we continue to think about those who are still seeking employment, we can also want more from work for ourselves. We must take a step away from the pain of surviving and take a bold step toward thriving—without the guilt.

ACTION PLANNER

What was the best job you've ever had? What made it so special for you?

_____

_____

_____

What was the worst job you've ever had? What needs of yours weren't being met?

_____

_____

_____

Think about your current job. What parts of your job give you the most satisfaction? Be as specific as possible.

_____

_____

_____

Using the "Twelve Factors of Job Satisfaction," indicate how important each one is for you and how well your current job is meeting those needs.

1. Money

For me, this is:

☐ Extremely important ☐ Somewhat important ☐ Not important

I am getting this need met:

☐ Very well ☐ Somewhat ☐ Not at all

2. Stability

For me, this is:

☐ Extremely important ☐ Somewhat important ☐ Not important

I am getting this need met:

☐ Very well ☐ Somewhat ☐ Not at all

3. Advancement

For me, this is:

☐ Extremely important ☐ Somewhat important ☐ Not important

I am getting this need met:

☐ Very well ☐ Somewhat ☐ Not at all

4. Recognition

For me, this is:
☐ Extremely important ☐ Somewhat important ☐ Not important

I am getting this need met:
☐ Very well ☐ Somewhat ☐ Not at all

5. Impact

For me, this is:
☐ Extremely important ☐ Somewhat important ☐ Not important

I am getting this need met:
☐ Very well ☐ Somewhat ☐ Not at all

6. Flow

For me, this is:
☐ Extremely important ☐ Somewhat important ☐ Not important

I am getting this need met:
☐ Very well ☐ Somewhat ☐ Not at all

7. Mastery

For me, this is:
☐ Extremely important ☐ Somewhat important ☐ Not important

I am getting this need met:
☐ Very well ☐ Somewhat ☐ Not at all

8. Autonomy

For me, this is:
☐ Extremely important ☐ Somewhat important ☐ Not important

I am getting this need met:
☐ Very well ☐ Somewhat ☐ Not at all

9. Expression

For me, this is:
☐ Extremely important ☐ Somewhat important ☐ Not important

I am getting this need met:
☐ Very well   ☐ Somewhat   ☐ Not at all

10. Physical Environment

For me, this is:
☐ Extremely important ☐ Somewhat important ☐ Not important

I am getting this need met:
☐ Very well   ☐ Somewhat   ☐ Not at all

11. Relationships

For me, this is:
☐ Extremely important ☐ Somewhat important ☐ Not important

I am getting this need met:
☐ Very well   ☐ Somewhat   ☐ Not at all

12. Work-Life Integration

For me, this is:
☐ Extremely important ☐ Somewhat important ☐ Not important

I am getting this need met:
☐ Very well   ☐ Somewhat   ☐ Not at all

Review your answers above. For those needs that are somewhat or extremely important to you and that are not being met as well as you would like, how could you more effectively meet those needs in your current job?

_____

_____

_____

_____

_____

For those needs that are somewhat or extremely important to you
and that are currently being met, what could you do on a daily basis
to keep them present for you?

_____

_____

_____

Converting from Living a Label to Living a Life

WHEN MY OLDER BROTHER, Scott, was a senior in college, he wrote home about the new woman he was dating. Three pieces of information stuck out: 1) she had the same first name as his sister (that's me), 2) she was from Minnesota (where's that?), and 3) she was Jewishly observant. While many Jewish families would have regarded that third detail as cause for either relief or celebration, our family took it as evidence that his new girlfriend was in a cult and would certainly try to get my brother to drink the (kosher) Kool-Aid.

While our family was Jewish, we were Jewish in label only. Any appearance of living a Jewish life was an unintended result of living in New York City, where you are practically Jewish just by living on its grid. We did have our own family traditions, of course: when faced with something we didn't really understand, we did what we always did—we made jokes. Not about Debra, Scott's girlfriend, of course. But about what we knew (or pretended to know) about living a committed Jewish life: a life that must be vacant without bacon, or stringent due to synagogue, or hamstrung by holidays that we didn't observe.

Over the years, as Scott and Debra's commitment to each other grew, our teasing waned out of respect for the challenges my brother faced in shifting from a Jewish label to a Jewish life. He was the one—not us—who would be keeping a kosher home. He was the one who would be blessing the wine and the challah each week. He was the one who would be raising his children to believe in a faith and a way of life he was only just learning about. And with what I'm sure were many concessions on both sides, Scott and Debra got married and are raising three bright, beautiful children who speak Hebrew, love Israel, lead synagogue services, and have their own well-developed opinions about what being Jewish means to them.

The Talmud tells us that "One person's candle is a light for many." Debra was that light for Scott, the two of them together lit up their three children to make their own Jewish connections, and they may be, in turn, the candle for others.

Ever competitive with my big brother, I dated a modern Orthodox man. This experience would turn out to be the "Jewish boot camp" that I never knew I wanted but am eternally grateful to have had. It's little wonder that the first family members to whom I introduced my new boyfriend were my brother and sister-in-law—a decision that saved me from a panic attack and my new flame from a wrongful arrest.

The first morning of our visit, I woke up and went downstairs to Scott and Debra's kitchen to feed my little niece, Shira, her breakfast. As I spooned scrambled eggs into her mouth, Shira stopped chewing long enough to point over my shoulder and ask, "Aunt Deborah, what's your friend doing?" I turned around to see my new friend slowly and painstakingly wrapping a black leather strap up his arm. I had seen enough *Afterschool Specials* on TV to associate this kind of activity with something illegal, immoral, or illicit. It was at the very moment that I was about to snatch my innocent niece from her highchair and run from the house that Debra came downstairs and explained to me the Jewish practice of laying tefillin—wrapping around one's arm and forehead straps to which are attached small black leather boxes containing parchment scrolls inscribed with verses from the Torah. I was humbled by how much I had to learn and relieved that I wouldn't have to turn my new boyfriend in to the cops.

The relationship didn't last, but what I had learned and begun to practice during our years together did. I learned how to *bentsh*—say prayers of thanks after meals—and how to talk to God. I learned a little Hebrew and a lot about keeping a kosher home. I learned how to be religiously observant of the Sabbath, and that I didn't want to. My candle flickered at times but was never extinguished.

All of these Jewish rites and rituals that I learned out of love paved the way for me to meet and marry my husband, Michael—who already kept a kosher home and had a relation- **I learned how** ship with God. His parents were his candles; **to be religiously** they gave him a light that keeps glowing—and **observant, and that** growing. Today, the two of us together have **I didn't want to** made a family of four who keep kosher, make Shabbat dinner, belong to a synagogue, and regard Jewish practice as a tenet of our daily lives. While Michael's flame was illuminated at birth (okay, maybe on day eight), and my flame was ignited in my twenties, I see that, in the eyes of our children, our lights have the same luster.

While Scott and Debra and Michael and I were busy keeping the home fires (of Judaism) burning, our newfound Jewish perspectives and practices were having an unintended effect on someone else: Mom. After marrying our stepfather, Ron, whose love of Judaism began early on, my mother started feeling a warm glow in her soul. That glow began to sparkle as my mom watched her thirteen grandchildren learn about and embrace Judaism. Those sparks turned into flames when my mom decided, at age sixty-two, to become a bat mitzvah. I will never forget watching my children watch their grandmother stand proudly on the *bimah,* knowing that they—at age seven—had already helped light someone else's candle.

On a trip to Los Angeles for work, I was delighted to have the opportunity to take my younger brother, Andrew, and his lovely girlfriend, Lourdes, out for a birthday dinner. As Andrew drove down the freeway, Lourdes and I got to know each other better. Born in Honduras, Lourdes was raised a Catholic. She was baptized, and received her first communion and confirmation, in the Catholic Church. Nevertheless, due to her openness to religion in general, it didn't seem strange for her to accept a coveted position as an early childhood educator at a Jewish community center.

"I just got back from a fantastic workshop," she told me, "where my supervisor and I learned how to apply *Pirkei Avot* in the classroom."

"*Pirkei A-what?*" my brother Andrew asked. "What's that?"

As Lourdes lovingly and correctly explained to her Jewish boyfriend the collection of rabbinical advice, ethics, and insights, I realized that I had the honor of watching the next of our siblings get curious about what Judaism could offer beyond worries and wars.

What will stick for Andrew? What will last? Who knows? I do know that when Andrew asked Lourdes if she would convert to Judaism when they got married, her response was "Will *you?*" She was challenging him to make his own commitment to something meaningful. Each of us—my two brothers and I—went on a Jewish journey in the name of love, and we have each moved along our own personal continuum ever since.

ACTION PLANNER

In reflecting on your religious or spiritual journey, who or what "lit your candle"? How so?

_____

_____

_____

_____

How have you made your journey uniquely your own?
What feels most like "you" about where you are today?

_____

_____

_____

_____

_____

What other parts of your spiritual or religious life would
you like to spark? What would that give you that you don't
already have?

_____

_____

_____

_____

_____

To whom can you turn or what can you do to generate
that spark?

_____

_____

_____

_____

_____

_____

What other parts of your personal life would you like to spark? What would that give you that you don't already have?

_____

_____

_____

_____

_____

To whom can you turn or what can you do to generate that spark?

_____

_____

_____

_____

_____

What parts of your professional life would you like to be sparked? What would that give you that you don't already have now?

_____

_____

_____

_____

_____

To whom can you turn or what can you do to generate that spark?

_____

_____

_____

_____

_____

Whose candle have you lit? How so? How do you know?

_____

_____

_____

_____

How does that make you feel?

_____

_____

_____

_____

_____

When Leadership Means Following

WHEN MY FATHER-IN-LAW gave my husband, Michael, and me a birthday gift of sessions with his personal trainer, I realized I had a choice: I could choose to be offended (was this a hint?) or I could choose to see this as an opportunity. Since I genuinely like my father-in-law, and he's not known for beating around the bush, I chose the latter. Michael and I booked our appointment with the trainer, Mona, and prepared to get ourselves into great shape. What I didn't know, but soon found out, was that the muscle most in need of this workout was my ego.

I am a take-charge kind of person—I run my own business, I make all of our family's social plans, and I like to achieve, accomplish, and yes, win. But within twenty minutes of crunching, squatting, and pushing-up with Michael and Mona, I was feeling like I wanted to lunge *at* them rather than *with* them. I was barely keeping up. I could not compete.

As much as I wanted to curl up into a child's pose (the only yoga move I've mastered because it requires little more than lying face-down in a ball on the floor and breathing), I wasn't permitted to. Mona made me get up and get moving. And I wasn't allowed to quit. My spirit was being crushed as I squeaked out a set of "skull-crushers" with a twelve-pound weight while balancing precariously on a stability ball. Why was the experience of being a learner so hard for me? Why was I so miserable?

Because I wasn't the leader. I had to follow. And when it comes to "going along with" rather than blazing the trail, my followership skills are as out of condition as the rest of me.

What was I even thinking? I was working with a professional trainer who was being paid to lead me. I was also working alongside Michael, who competes in triathlons—for fun! There was no way that I was going to be the best, the strongest, the boss. Heck, I was lucky that I was even allowed to be a part of this party. Learning to follow was going to be a bigger workout for my head, heart, and soul than I had anticipated.

Perhaps this little problem sounds familiar to you. We are bombarded with messages that tell us the who, what, where, when, **The muscle most in need of this workout was my ego** why, and how of leadership. My bookshelf is filled with tomes from leadership gurus. These books teach us how to step up, stand out, take charge, and march ahead in a way that compels others to follow. And their messages about how to lead are indeed gripping.

Among my favorites are James Kouzes and Barry Posner in *Leadership Challenge:* "Leaders must know where they are going if they expect others to willingly join them on the journey." Stephen Covey wrote in his book *The 7 Habits of Highly Effective People,* "Effective leadership is putting first things first," and Sam Walton commented in his autobiography, *Sam Walton,* "High expectations are the key to everything." Rabbi Nachman of Bratslav conveyed, "When a man is able to take abuse with a smile, he is worthy to become a leader."

As a self-defined and self-appointed leader, I strive to do all of the above. Yet former Speaker of the House Sam Rayburn adds another skill set to the mix, as he is known for saying: "You cannot be a leader, and ask other people to follow you, unless you know how to follow, too." That's a new perspective for many of us—whether we are in official positions of leadership or struggle with the fact that we're not. Either way, learning to step back and abide by someone else's plan is part of leadership, and, frankly, part of life. It's a part of life that I struggle with—whether that person with a plan is my trainer, my colleague, or a family member.

I don't recall Daniel H. Pink interviewing me for his book, *Drive: The Surprising Truth about What Motivates Us.* However, as I read it, I was struck by the similarities between my desire to call all the shots and Pink's observation that autonomy—acting from a place of choice—is critically linked to personal and professional well-being.

Pink breaks these needs down into the four Ts of autonomy— "autonomy over task," "autonomy over time," "autonomy over team," and "autonomy over technique," each of which helps us understand where we may want more of a leadership role in work and life—and where we may want or need to follow others.

1. People want to have a say in what they do.

If remembering everything in your life hinges on strategically placed Post-it Notes, then you owe a debt of gratitude to the idea of autonomy over task. In the early 1970s, 3M researcher Spencer Silver was working in the laboratory (having been granted autonomy over task), trying to create a strong adhesive. What he developed was a weak adhesive that stuck to objects and could easily be lifted off. 3M considered this a useless discovery and stripped him of his autonomy over the task. His loss, however, was the world's gain: the failed adhesive became the basis for 3M's Press'n'Peel pads—the precursor to the Post-it Note. At that point, the company's president and chairman, William McKnight, established a policy that 3M's technical staff could spend up to 15 percent of their time on any project that struck their fancy. In other words, McKnight granted everyone autonomy over task. Despite its origins, giving people autonomy over task isn't always an idea that

45

sticks. Many leaders feel that their job is to tell people exactly what to do so that their tasks align with departmental or organizational goals. As accountability becomes more important, leaders fear (for good reason) that it will be their butts on the line if their team fails to accomplish its objectives. I don't disagree. I am a huge advocate of managers communicating clear goals for their staff that are aligned with business objectives—and managing expectations all along the way. However, when employees have no control over any part of their duties, they may toe the line while dragging their feet. What you get is following from a place of compliance rather than a place of commitment—which yields uninspired work and workers. If what your workplace needs is a booster shot of energy, excitement, and innovation, you might consider offering employees more autonomy over task if you're the boss, or advocating for it if you're not. (Perhaps you could write down your request on a Post-it as an opener.)

2. People want to have a say in when the work gets done.

There is an appointed time for everything, a time for every event under heaven:

A time to give birth, and a time to die; a time to plant, and a time to uproot what is planted.

A time to kill, and a time to heal; a time to tear down, and a time to build up.

A time to weep, and a time to laugh; a time to mourn, and a time to dance....

Whether these words remind you of Pete Seeger, the Byrds, or the Bible, if you are managing or being managed in alignment with these sentiments, you are in strict violation of autonomy over time. When we are told exactly when to do every single part of our jobs, we feel as if we are working on a factory line—or worse—back in elementary school. Giving people choice and control over time—not all of it, but enough to make them want to show up and follow your lead—is Kryptonite to micromanagement.

In their book, *Why Work Sucks and How to Fix It,* authors Cali Ressler and Jody Thompson contend that "we all labor under a myth: Time + Physical Presence = Results." They go on to write, "With the exception of sales people, who either deliver their numbers or don't, most people are judged by a mixture of results and time spent in the office. You are expected to do your job and complete your tasks, but you are also expected to put in forty hours or even more."

That sounds like most work environments I know, except that "forty or even more" feels like a gross understatement. But Ressler and Thompson make a critical case for giving people autonomy over time when they observe:

> If you're out running errands on Saturday and getting things done, you're not measuring yourself by the clock. You might be frustrated that a specific chore is taking so long, but you don't look at a pile of laundry and think, I'd better make sure that I'm putting enough hours into this. You either accomplish what you set out to accomplish or you don't. If anything, there is incentive to get things done more quickly and efficiently because then you'll have more time to do something else. At work, even if we accomplish our tasks, we are expected to fill the hours.

Workplaces that put such tight controls over time hinder rather than help work outcomes and work satisfaction. With this in mind, Ressler and Thompson developed the ROWE (Results-Only Work Environment) philosophy, famously put in place by Best Buy. The big idea? Pay employees for their productivity, not the hours they spend at work. Best Buy employees are leaders when it comes to control over time, and followers of a philosophy and management style that they have come to embrace because of the autonomy it grants them.

The Harvard Business Review reported about Best Buy that "Salaried people put in as much time as it takes to do their work. Hourly employees in the program work a set number of hours to comply with federal labor regulations, but they get to choose when. Those employees report better relationships with family and friends, more company loyalty, and more focus and energy....Employees don't know whether they work fewer hours—they've stopped counting."

What was that again? Most of us stop counting hours only on weekends or vacations, except toward the end, when we begin counting the hours until we have to go back to work. Can you imagine a workplace that's more focused on getting the objectives met than the amount of time you have to spend creating the appearance that you're working hard on those objectives? It's radical, I know. But in a very real way, giving people autonomy over time so that they can accomplish what needs to be done—and then take some time to recharge, renew, or even re-energize for the next project—is as practical as it is radical.

3. People want to have a say in whom they work with.

Cain and Abel. Jacob and Esau. Joseph and all of his brothers. These guys didn't have any choice about whom they toiled next to in the fields day after day—and I ask you to consider how well that worked out for them. While you may not have interpersonal conflicts of biblical proportions, chances are you have people with whom you prefer to work and those whom you prefer to keep at a respectful distance.

In his book, *The Leader's Guide to Radical Management,* Stephen Denning offers research that shows many high-performance teams are self-organized rather than manager led. He writes, "They were teams where the management had deliberately stepped back, or was inattentive...thus enabling the team to self-organize. It's as though there was a tear in the fabric of the universe, an open space that was created, and lo and behold, the self-organizing team emerged."

I have to assume that most managers (and even most direct reports) would not eagerly embrace a tear-in-the-fabric-of-the-universe style of work. However, managers should keep this basic advice in mind from entrepreneur extraordinaire Mary Kay Ash: "Pretend that every single person you meet has a sign around his or her neck that says, 'Make me feel important.' Not only will you succeed in sales, you will succeed in life." What most organizations could do better is give people the opportunity to work with teammates who make them feel important, valued, and respected—and teach people how to communicate and demonstrate these sentiments. Giving people choice and appreciation is how we recognize and retain the talent we've already invested in.

Of course, even self-directed, self-selecting teams can experience a crisis, and when that happens, how they handle the crisis can become a catalyst for relationship building. As Oprah Winfrey put it, "Lots of people want to ride with you in the limo, but what you want is someone who will take the bus with you when the limo breaks down."

4. People want to have a say in how they accomplish the work.

In his book, *War as I Knew It,* General George S. Patton makes a powerful statement in favor of giving people control over how they carry out their mission: "Never tell people how to do things. Tell them what to do and they will surprise you with their ingenuity." While Patton might have been bumping up against the drive for autonomy over task ("tell them what to do"), he makes a powerful statement in favor of giving people control over how they carry out their mission.

Zappos.com, the online retailer, is an example of a company that gives its employees autonomy over technique. Pink writes of Zappos's customer service staff, "When a call comes in, here's their job: Serve the customer. No scripts. No monitoring. No timing of calls either. If a call takes one minute, great; if it takes one hour, no problem." The powerful, positive results of this autonomy over task include minimal staff turnover and an exceptional reputation for customer service.

One of my coaching clients, Daniel, wanted his customer service staff to operate like Zappos as well, but was running up against a barrier he couldn't identify. Daniel's company provides twenty-four-hour comprehensive technical support to medical offices, and his natural hands-off management style seemed like a good fit for his staff. His employees were often given complex assignments, such as running client reports sorted by dozens of distinct variables, and they were granted lots of leeway as to how they handled them. Seasoned staff appreciated the freedom they had to employ their own creative problem-solving techniques. But interviews with newer staff members revealed that they actually felt hindered by the freedom granted to them. While they appreciated not being micromanaged, they felt lost because they were given more choice and control than they knew what to do with so early in their employment. While autonomy over technique served their more seasoned colleagues, it was getting in the way of the newer employees' ability to learn the basics.

My job was to help Daniel understand that giving people the freedom to approach work and solve problems as they saw fit was something that needed to be earned over time. It was warranted only after employees demonstrated a solid understanding of the business; could follow its processes, policies, procedures, and systems; and could identify the clients' full range of needs and expectations. They needed to practice as followers first. For Daniel, this meant that he would need to be more hands-on with new hires until they were ready for him to take a finger off, then another, then another, until the timing was right for his hands-off management style to take effect.

Whether you're talking about autonomy over time, task, team, or technique, one thing is clear: control and choice in the workplace are earned. These are privileges, not birthrights. Even when someone is described as "a natural-born leader," that often refers to charisma rather than competence. Until any one of us has proven that we know how to manage our time, complete tasks exceptionally well, think innovatively, and work well with others, we will need to follow the leadership of someone who has earned his or her autonomy and can grant us ours—when and if the time is right.

ACTION PLANNER

What is your definition of leadership?

_____

_____

_____

What is your definition of "followership"?

_____

_____

_____

Where in your life do leadership and followership come into play? Where do they come into conflict?

_____

_____

_____

In which aspects of your work and life does having control feel most important to you?

_____

_____

_____

In general, how much autonomy do you feel that you have?

	At work	At home	Other _____
Autonomy over what I do	☐ Too much ☐ Just the right amount ☐ Could use more ☐ None at all	☐ Too much ☐ Just the right amount ☐ Could use more ☐ None at all	☐ Too much ☐ Just the right amount ☐ Could use more ☐ None at all
Autonomy over when I get to do it	☐ Too much ☐ Just the right amount ☐ Could use more ☐ None at all	☐ Too much ☐ Just the right amount ☐ Could use more ☐ None at all	☐ Too much ☐ Just the right amount ☐ Could use more ☐ None at all
Autonomy over whom I get to work with	☐ Too much ☐ Just the right amount ☐ Could use more ☐ None at all	☐ Too much ☐ Just the right amount ☐ Could use more ☐ None at all	☐ Too much ☐ Just the right amount ☐ Could use more ☐ None at all
Autonomy over how I get the work done	☐ Too much ☐ Just the right amount ☐ Could use more ☐ None at all	☐ Too much ☐ Just the right amount ☐ Could use more ☐ None at all	☐ Too much ☐ Just the right amount ☐ Could use more ☐ None at all

Review your answers above. In which areas of your life do you want more or less autonomy than you have? How would having more or less choice/control better serve you?

If I had more choice or control in this area...	I would have/feel/be able to...

If I had more choice or control in this area...	I would have/feel/be able to...

Which of those areas above are within your control to change? Which are not?

_____

_____

_____

_____

For those areas within your control, what is the first step you can take toward changing your current situation (such as talking to your boss, getting additional training, finding a mentor)?

_____

_____

_____

_____

For those areas outside of your control, what do you need to let go of (such as not being able to choose your project team members or change the deadline for an upcoming report)?

_____

_____

_____

_____

For those areas in which you'd like to lead more and follow less, write down what you've done so far to earn your autonomy (such as, "I have consistently met my project deadlines for the past two years, so I'd like to be able to decide my projects' timelines and deadlines moving forward").

_____

_____

_____

_____

_____

If you can't change your current situation, what single small element *can* you change?

_____

_____

_____

_____

Who in your work or home life has earned some more autonomy—more choice/control—than you are giving them credit for? How will you acknowledge this and grant them the autonomy that they have earned?

_____

_____

_____

_____

6

There's No Time Like the Present to Unwrap Your Gifts

IF I WERE a doctor or a lawyer, I might not get asked this question as often as I do: "How did you get into this line of work?" Apparently, to some folks, there's something quixotic, exotic, or perhaps idiotic about someone who speaks publicly for a living.

So here's the deal: Rumor has it that I was born loud. Before turning six, I asked my mother for a microphone for my birthday, and, according to family lore, my older brother got down on bended knee, begging her to ignore my request. While every report card I got in grade school and middle school reflected my academic prowess, they also indicated my gift of gab (although not necessarily using "gifted" terminology). Once I entered New York City's Stuyvesant High School, I was immediately drafted for a team that develops and rewards those of us who are elite athletes from the neck up: The Speech and Debate Team. At the end of my senior year of high school, after three years spent travelling around North America competing against other mouthy masterminds, I won the national championship in original oration. So, starting at age seventeen, I began doing presentation skills training at colleges and then corporations, and I'm still doing that today.

In the words of one client, "You're like the Doogie Howser of public speaking!" Thanks... I think.

With over twenty years of speaking experience under my belt, I feel that I know what I'm doing. But more importantly, I know for sure that I'm doing what I was meant to be doing. I've taken a natural strength and interest, and turned it into a career.

Like most of us, I had a few talents and interests as a kid, but not all of them were worth pursuing as an adult. I managed to unearth a particular natural gift; water it with time, energy, practice, and attention; keep it in the light; and my vocation was born. I'm doing something so "me" that I can't imagine what my life would have looked like without this element. It's the career equivalent of marrying your high-school sweetheart: sometimes, the right match comes along earlier than you could have imagined. I realize every day that finding and falling in love with the right job early in life is a supreme blessing that I have been given, and it all started with a God-given and home-grown gift.

Each of us came into this world with a rainbow of natural colors that we once honored and delighted in before we were saddled with the responsibilities of adulthood. Maybe you were innately coordinated, like my daughter, Sophie, is. When people ask, "What's her sport?" we answer, "Whatever she decides it is."

But here's the tricky part: she has big dreams of becoming a professional basketball player with the WNBA. It's possible; anything is possible. There are a few barriers, of course, most notably the slim odds of anyone becoming a professional athlete. Whether or not Sophie becomes the Jewish Maya Moore or Sheryl Swoopes, I predict that she will honor her natural gifts—her coordination and strength—throughout her life. It gives her pleasure, reward, and challenge. Basketball doesn't have to become her career for her to reap the benefits of staying physically active, strong, and fit. As long as she continues to enjoy and develop her gifts, then, from my perspective, it's a slam dunk.

Beth, the owner of a small construction management business, came to me to help her manage her time more effectively. Beth was convinced that she would get more done each day if she could just find a single time-management system that worked for her. Beth was an avid reader and had already read many of my favorite books on time management: Stephen Covey's *The 7 Habits of Highly Effective People,* Timothy Ferriss's *The 4-Hour Workweek,* and *Eat That Frog!* by Brian Tracy. In addition to her voracious reading habits, Beth was helping her local office supply store stay in business by purchasing most (if not all) of the calendar and scheduling systems they stocked. From whiteboards to Post-it Notes to day planners to desk blotters, Beth had them all. She had tried at least twenty different systems— and was frustrated with the clutter on her desk and in her mind. She wanted *the* system.

As much as Beth wanted me to prescribe a course of treatment for her time-management challenges, I sensed that she needed to learn more about her natural gifts before we picked a plan. I asked Beth a fundamental question that Marcus Buckingham suggests in his 2005 *Harvard Business Review* article, "What Great Managers Do": "What was the best day at work you've had in the last three months?" Beth answered my question with a question, "How can I answer that? Every day is so different around here!"

The day sounded like a kitchen-sink sundae—a scoop of every flavor of activity possible

"I know," I answered. "See if one terrific day stands out in particular."

Beth grew silent as she thought about it. "Okay, I've got it." And she began to describe a day that sounded like a "kitchen-sink sundae"—a little scoop of every flavor of activity possible. On her "best day," Beth woke up early and made it to the gym and back in time to drive her three children to school. When she arrived at work, she finished up a proposal that had been weighing on her since the deadline was rapidly approaching. After that, she went on a sales call that yielded her a new client, surprised her husband by taking him out to lunch, and then went back to the office to have a status meeting with her project management team. When her best friend called to ask if she could skip out for a quick cup of coffee, Beth gladly did so, and returned to work to pay some bills and send some invoices. Beth made it home for dinner, drove her daughter to soccer practice and back, and then logged back on to the computer to do some remaining work before settling into bed with her husband and a book.

"What made this day stand out for you?" I asked Beth.

"It was that I was able to get all of those things done—the work, the family time, the "me" time—and not have to stick to a plan. I just knew what I needed to do and did it, and I also was able to throw in a couple of surprises and make all of those work out, too."

"So, it was your flexibility that made the day so great?" I asked to clarify.

"Yes!" Beth concurred. "I loved that I could be so adaptable and make everything work."

"So, the flexibility piece is really important to you, is that right?"

"Yes. That's what I love about having my own business. The flexibility. My clients like that I can and will accommodate them—I'm not rigid. My staff appreciates that I allow them plenty of flexibility as well. I can run the shop this way without being unpredictable or scattered or a pushover. I've found the right balance."

"So it sounds!" I reaffirmed. "And so, Beth, I am curious. You have this incredible knack for being flexible. You are getting things done on your terms and on your schedule. It's why you love your job—and your life."

"Absolutely!" Beth substantiated. "One hundred percent."

"So tell me again about what you want from a single time-management system. What do you want it to give you that you don't have now?"

"I guess I want it to give me a structure." And then she laughed.

"What's funny, Beth?"

"I just realized that I have been banging my head against the wall trying to find something that will give me the very thing I don't want!"

"I don't want more structure. I'm great at operating without external guidelines and rules. I know how to stay nimble and get things done. I'm really good at it."

"It's one of your gifts, right?"

"Absolutely!" Beth replied.

"So what's going on here? Why the drive to find a time-management system to put you in a box—or make you check off boxes—when you operate so well outside the box?" I asked.

"I guess I already have my own time-management system. And it works. It just doesn't look like anyone else's. Heck, it doesn't even look the same from day to day. But I am getting things done and done well," Beth said with pride.

Dedicate your time, energy, and resources to improving what you are already good at

"I am thinking that's ridiculous and that I need to accept that I have one already, and it's working. And I created it myself!" Beth announced.

"Yes you did! Congratulations on that. And maybe one day you could market "Beth's Time-Management System for Flexible Entrepreneurs!" I suggested.

"Only if I could explain it!" Beth laughed.

But even if she couldn't explain it, Beth already had a system that was working for her. And it was a system that was working for her because it was formulated organically around her gift: flexibility.

It isn't enough to merely identify what you're good at—you need to put those strengths into action. In addition, it's important to keep in mind that you will get further faster by focusing on fortifying what's working well rather than spending time overcoming your weaknesses. Too often, people dedicate their improvement efforts to areas in which they are entirely incompetent. Instead, dedicate your time, energy, and resources to improving what you are already good at. According to Peter Drucker in his article, "Managing Oneself,"

"It takes far more energy to improve from incompetence to mediocrity than to improve from first-rate performance to excellence." I'd rather conserve my energy for other things, wouldn't you?

Of course, that doesn't mean that we should be blind to our limitations. Buckingham contends that when you only see your gifts, it's easy to develop an inflated view of your own capabilities. You want to be confident without being reckless or cocky. To stay focused on your gifts while still maintaining a healthy sense of humility, bear in mind the size, scope, and challenges of the goals ahead. Drucker reminds us that it's valuable to concentrate and capitalize on our strengths, as long as we can see where we might need help along the way.

Many of us don't give ourselves the gift of time or attention to see who we are when we are at our best, using the strengths that we were born with—or that we've developed over time. Poet Denise Levertov wrote in *Work that Enfaiths:* "Invisible wings are given to us too, by which, if we would dare to acknowledge and use them, we might transcend the dualities of time and matter—might be upheld to walk on water." The great Chasidic rebbe and teacher, Zusya, believed that at the end of his life, he would be asked to give a reckoning and inventory of how he used his gifts. He knew that he wouldn't be asked, "Why weren't you more like Moses?" Nor would he be asked, "Why weren't you more like Abraham?" He anticipated that he would be asked, "Why weren't you more like Zusya?" In other words, he would be held accountable for how much of his natural gifts he was able to bring to life, to use to enrich the world and the people around him.

If you've been waiting for the end of your days to ask yourself, "How could I have been more 'me' during my life?" then you've been waiting too long. Whether you could use a new career, a new hobby, or a new perspective, think back to your natural gifts. It's time to honor who you really were—and still are.

ACTION PLANNER

What were your favorite activities as a kid? What did you love about those activities?

_____

_____

_____

What were you known for doing well?

_____

_____

_____

What made you feel most proud? Excited? Engaged?

_____

_____

_____

When did you stop doing these activities? Why?

_____

_____

_____

_____

What parts of these activities are you still engaged in, personally or professionally?

_____

_____

_____

What activities have you abandoned that you'd like to revisit?

_____

_____

_____

What gifts do you know you still have? How do you know?

_____

_____

_____

What was the best day you had at work in the last three months? What made it so memorable?

_____

_____

_____

_____

_____

_____

What gifts were you using on your best day?

_____

_____

_____

_____

How can you use these gifts on a more regular basis?

_____

_____

_____

_____

How can you develop these gifts even more?

_____

_____

_____

_____

When will you get started?

_____

_____

_____

_____

Get Along with Others

Open Mouth, Insert Foot:
Let Your Ears Hear What Your Lips Speak

WHEN I MET my husband more than a decade ago, we both knew within the first two weeks that this was *it*. So it didn't feel like we were rushing things when he asked me to meet his parents after only one month of dating.

Despite an excellent track record of having wooed and won over my boyfriends' parents through the years, I was nervous. This time the stakes felt higher. As we drove the three hours to Michael's parents' summer home on Long Island during heavy Friday traffic, I coped with my nerves the best way I could: by telling jokes. Three hours of smiling and laughing had to be better than three hours of *shvitzing* (sweating) and *tsuris* (aggravation), right? I pulled out all the stops: favorite bits from my college stand-up comedy routine, old Borscht Belt gags, painful groaners, and one positively filthy and universally offensive joke from George Carlin. What can I say? I was in love and I had three hours to fill.

By the time we were halfway through Shabbat dinner that night, I had relaxed. Michael and I shared a secret victory smile and played a quick game of footsie under the table. At a natural lull in the conversation, Michael piped up: "Deb, why don't you tell my parents that joke you told me on the car ride?"

All told, I had probably shared fifty jokes on the ride. Which one did he mean?

"You know," Michael pressed, with a glimmer of mischief in his eyes, "*that* one!"

I could think of only one joke that would qualify for that level of naughty nuance. So, emboldened by romance and red wine, I proceeded to recount one of George Carlin's dirtiest lines to my new boyfriend's parents.

It wasn't until the last words were exiting my mouth that I made eye contact with Michael again, and when I did, I saw that his face had drained of all color and his mouth had gone slack. The room was silent, save for the crickets outside chirping their evening song. As I sat there in stony silence, looking at Michael's horrified parents who were looking anywhere but at me, Michael recovered his power of speech long enough to croak: "I didn't mean that one."

I learned a valuable lesson about knowing your audience before you say a word

Too little, too late—and at a big cost. How big? Let's put it this way: By the end of the weekend, Michael's dad had pulled aside his single, thirty-year-old Jewish son and recommended that he not rush into settling down—the first and last conversation of this kind in history.

Fast forward more than a dozen years: The good news is we've all recovered from my debacle. The better news is my in-laws don't even remember it. The best news is that I learned a valuable lesson about knowing your audience before you say a word. And as usual, all of this news is old news. As we are warned in Bereishit, the first book of the Torah, "Let your ears hear what your lips speak." It also seems critical to let your ears hear what your lips speak before you speak it, and also keep in mind that your ears are not the only ones listening.

Knowing your audience is a critical competency for anyone who presents ideas—and that's every single one of us. Whether your goal is to close a deal, solicit a donation, sell a concept, overcome an objection, teach a new behavior, secure a client, or win a heart, you need to be aware that your listeners come with their own set of assumptions, expectations, hopes, and fears about you and the topic you're discussing.

Chances are you do this already without even thinking about it. When you've put together a cost-benefit analysis for your boss, you've considered your audience's needs. The same goes for when you send your company's CEO to meet with a potential client who only wants to work with the top brass. And when my kids ask their grandma if they can stay up late to watch another episode of *Sponge Bob* while they gobble from their tureens of ice cream—a request that would never, ever fly with the home team—they're doing it too.

But when you have a new audience, you can't simply rely on what's worked in the past. Every single time I prepare to facilitate a workshop, deliver a keynote speech, or even have a one-on-one with a new client, I think about (and where possible, ask ahead of time) what this particular audience wants and needs to hear and how they want to hear it. Yes, even if I have spoken about this exact topic before, and yes, even if I have coached someone with this same issue before. New person + new approach = custom-fit results. And as you know, I learned this lesson the hard way.

Communications consultant Nick Morgan writes in *Give Your Speech, Change the World* that there are five audience dimensions to consider before making a formal presentation or even having an informal conversation to share ideas: "openness vs. closed," "powerful vs. subservient," "engaged vs. disengaged," "allied vs. opposed," and "committed vs. uncommitted." So here are five questions to ask about your audience before you go full-steam ahead:

1. **"If I knock on their door, will they let me in?"** How receptive is this audience likely to be to new ideas? How receptive is this audience likely to be to you? If your listeners tend to be closed off to new people or new ideas, you may need to frame the introduction of any novel approach as an extension of something they already know or are comfortable with. For example, when I train people to be solicitors for philanthropic

organizations, I help them brainstorm language that will move "closed" donors and prospects to "openness." I suggest starting a conversation with, "I'd like to fill you in on all the ways in which your last generous donation made a meaningful difference and hear what you're thinking about for this year." This is honest and gentle—like a friendly knock on a neighbor's door—which is much more welcome than showing up with your screwdriver to take the door off the hinges. Keep in mind, however, that even when your audience is already open, you need to keep the trust and connection going, because an open door can easily slam shut.

2. **"Who's really in charge here?"** It's critical to consider all of the power relationships in the room. When I teach workshops on supervision skills, I recognize that there is a different kind of participation in the session when supervisors and their direct reports take the class together than when they are in two separate workshops. While training these two groups together can and often does lead to better sharing of ideas, communication of expectations, and two-way feedback, it can also quash honest dialogue. Supervisees worry that they can't truly share their challenges when their boss is in the room for fear of retribution. To work with this very real dynamic, I often have participants share questions, concerns, or requests in writing—and without identifying personal information. When everyone in the group—managers and direct reports—is looking at the same list of challenges, it can depersonalize the feedback, making it feel safer to discuss "hypotheticals" rather than "personals."

3. **"What's our connection here?"** If this is a new audience, how can you help them feel connected to you? If the audience

is familiar, how can you enhance the connection you already have? As a speaker working with Jewish organizations, I often share personal stories about myself and my family, Jewish holidays, rituals, celebrations, etc. Why? Because I know that the "J-factor" is one we have in common, no matter how much variation there may be in how we observe or practice. That commonality creates cohesion between me and my listeners, helping us to engage with each other. Any new ideas and approaches I share have a greater likelihood of sticking. When I speak with my corporate audiences, I minimize the "J-factor" and maximize the "B-factor"—business relevance. In order to get these listeners on board and involved, I make the case early and often for how what I am telling them will make their jobs and their lives easier.

4. **"Who's (already) on my side?"** When considering allies versus opponents, we need to consider how much this audience already agrees with us and our point of view. The name of your topic is a tool that can be used to attract or repel. One of my most frequently requested training sessions is the strategically titled, "Oh [BLEEP!] Another Meeting???" Yes, I could have called it simply "Meeting Management" or "How to Run a Meeting." However, by naming the workshop after a perspective with which the vast majority of attendees already agree, I have created a room of allies. All those opposed? They are welcome, too, of course, and then I invite them to share their unique and valuable perspective on why they love meetings so much. Furthermore, my giving them so much attention and recognition makes them allies in this meeting, too! What do you do when you face a room of opposition? You spend some time genuinely and generously acknowledging their current perspective, making them feel right, heard, and understood,

before you even attempt to share a new perspective. So while I might believe that meetings provide an incomparable forum for building support, generating buy-in, and creating social capital, I don't start there. I start where my audience is. To quote author Dave Barry from his book, *Dave Barry Turns 50:* "If you had to identify, in one word, the reason why the human race has not achieved, and never will achieve, its full potential, that word would be *meetings*."

5. **"Did they bring their WIIFMs with them?"** How much buy-in to you or your ideas does this audience already have? If you're lucky, you'll have a group of listeners who have already bought into your point of view and are ready to take action. This group has already brought their WIIFMs ("What's In It for Me?") with them, and they're clear about why they're there and what they hope to get out of the training. When I tell my son, Jacob, a preternaturally gifted chef (or "Iron Chef Junior," as he prefers to be called), to turn off the television because we need to go to the grocery store, it doesn't take a hard sell to get him moving—especially when I give him time to find a recipe he wants to tackle and offer to get the ingredients for it on our excursion. He's already committed—and ready to go. However, when I make the same request to turn off the television so we can go on a bike ride or walk the local track, I know that I am in for resistance. When dealing with an uncommitted audience, you'll need to identify and name the right WIIFM for these particular listeners.

Whether you're making a pitch to a new client, proposing a personal or organizational change, or even meeting the parents, you'll want to make sure that you follow the counsel of the thirteenth-century poet Immanuel ben Solomon of Rome: "Keep silent or speak wisely."

ACTION PLANNER

Before you say a word, use the space below to get to know those whom you wish to engage—whether it's a single person, a group of people, or even your future in-laws:

1. What do I know about my audience personally and professionally that will impact how I present my ideas (age, gender, cultural background, education, job responsibility and status, civic and religious affiliation, etc.)?

_____

_____

_____

_____

_____

2. What do they already assume about this topic? About me?

_____

_____

_____

3. What does my audience already know about this topic? About me?

_____

_____

_____

_____

4. What previous experiences (positive, negative, neutral, or unknown) has my audience already had with this topic? With me?

_____

_____

_____

5. What does my audience want or hope for?

_____

_____

_____

6. What is my audience worried about?

_____

_____

_____

7. What are their hot buttons or sensitivities? Should I address or avoid these?

_____

_____

_____

8. What do they really need to take away from this conversation or presentation?

_____

_____

_____

Let It Rip!

TEMPORARILY LOSING my left eyebrow changed me permanently.

As I entered the salon, I should have wondered if a seven-dollar procedure might not have rigorous safety measures in place. All I saw were the posters on the wall showcasing lustrous legs and burnished bikini lines. By the time I might have thought this through more carefully, the salon lady had already applied a gluey glob of hot wax to my face, let it set, and, with a flex of her toned bicep, ripped it off. With an inch of eyebrow attached. The part I had been planning to keep.

Upon seeing her handiwork, the horrified woman let out a gasp and reflexively adopted the universal pose of people in the face of catastrophe: she covered her mouth with her hand. Nevertheless, her hand couldn't silence the words slowly leaking from it: "Sorrysorrysorrysorrysorry!"

My hand flew to my newly denuded brow, and, after a moment of shock, an odd calm settled inside me. My caretaker instinct took over, and I told the now shaking semi-aesthetician that it was just an accident, and not to worry—these things happen and eyebrows grow back. Then I peeled off some bills (including a tip by force of habit), handed them over, and headed home.

When I walked in the house, Michael greeted me in the front hall. I set my shoulders back and held my head up imperiously, daring him to laugh at my expense. He took the dare. I walked past him into the kitchen, where our twins, Jacob and Sophie, were sorting fruit snacks by color, shape, and size. "Hi guys!" I said with casual abandon. Jacob looked up at me, and, with an expression of bewilderment and bemusement on his face, asked "What happened to your eyebrow?" You can always count on your kids to say it like it is.

Sophie, not one to normally be distracted from a snack or from a sorting activity (let alone a project that involved both), snapped her head up. She just stared at me—now *that* was worse than Jacob's question. Gathering what was left of my dignity, I calmly explained how the lady at the nail place had had a small accident involving my left eyebrow, and that in time, it would grow back. Sophie took this in, smiled, and got an expectant twinkle in her eye. "How mad did you get?"

Ah. Redemption time.

"Honey, I didn't get mad. I was calm and polite. After all, what good would yelling do?" I boasted of my atypical calm in the face of defacement.

Bad move.

"What?" demanded Sophie. "You didn't get mad? About *that?"*

I knew exactly what Sophie was referring to. She was recalling:

- All the times that I snapped at her for leaving a blue blob of toothpaste in the sink.

- All the times that I raised my voice at her for taking too long to choose a stuffed animal for a trip.

- All the times that I screeched about her chewing with her mouth open.

Sophie was remembering all the times I had lost my cool with someone I adore—for minor annoyances, mind you—and now that an imperfect perfect stranger had *ripped off my eyebrow,* I didn't so much as bat an eyelash. (Which, thankfully, I still had.)

"What good would yelling do?" I asked her, and myself as well.

As I waited for my eyebrow to grow back, I had plenty of time to reflect on the triggers, hot buttons, and slights that usually prompted me to react with anger. These included:

- Lateness (I can manage my time—why can't you manage yours?)

- Hinting (You've got something to say? Say it directly!)

- Whining (You've got something to say? Say it, but without that tone!)

- Lateness (My time is valuable to me, and it should be valuable to you, too.)

> *You can always count on your kids to tell it like it is*

- "Laundry-bagging" (I can take criticism, but don't bring up everything I've ever done that bugs you.)

- Lateness (Did I mention this already?)

In addition to identifying these behaviors, I also realized that I was less likely to react negatively to a single offense (for which, I hoped, the eyebrow situation qualified) than to repeat occurrences of offensive behavior (such a leaving toothpaste in the sink over and over and over again). In other words, I would rather be unpleasantly surprised once than repeatedly ignored.

But more importantly, I would rather be better equipped to manage my responses in any situation. And in order to look forward to acquiring new and better behaviors in the face of frustration, I first had to look back. Way back. *Pirkei Avot (The Ethics of the Fathers)* chapter 5 tells us, "There are four types of temperaments. One who is quick to anger and quick to calm down—his gain is outweighed by his loss. One who is slow to anger and slow to calm down—his loss is outweighed by his gain. One who is slow to anger and quick to calm down is pious. One who is quick to anger and slow to calm down is wicked."

I realized that I probably fell somewhere between loser and wicked. Just as God had hardened Pharaoh's heart to the cries of the Israelites and his own people, I had hardened my words far too often,

What triggers, hot buttons, and slights prompt you to react with anger? when what I really needed to do was soften my approach. Each of us chooses how we react to situations, states of mind, and people. Even though our responses feel automatic, when we can recognize our triggers, we can slow down our responses, consider our options, then choose what to say—or not to say.

How can we do that? By identifying what sets us off, recognizing what we can and can't control, communicating our expectations to others, and ultimately, taking responsibility for our reactions and responses.

Gail, a senior vice president of a pharmaceutical company, was letting it rip on a regular basis, excoriating staff members in private and public. After two years, she was under considerable pressure from both her staff and the CEO to temper her temper. When I was called in to help Gail manage her reactions, I was told that her job was on the line. Without consistent, observable changes to her behavior, Gail would be fired.

The good news was that Gail was not about to deny any of the claims—she readily and easily admitted that there were plenty of situations that triggered her rage. We quickly got to work identifying her hot buttons:

- Staff members who brought her incomplete work she felt they could have finished or corrected on their own.

- Staff members who left work earlier in the day than she believed they should (like at 5:00 p.m.).

- Staff members who were slow to complete work.

- Staff members who expected praise for good work rather than exceptional work.

- Staff members whom she considered disloyal to her or to the company.

After the "what," our next step was to identify the "when." When were her reactions most intense? First thing in the morning? After a long day? When she was hungry?

Her answer was eye-opening: When she was bored. Because Gail was so goal-oriented and driven, having mental downtime was anathema to her. When Gail got bored, she got creative—creative in mining for trouble. Gail's "aha!" moment was the impetus for us to get creative in both managing the boredom and her reactions. I asked Gail, who had been happily married for almost thirty years, whether she had the same scorching retorts at home when she felt angry or bored. Gail laughed, "Not at all!" When I pressed her to explain what she did at home to keep her temper in check, she told me that she simply washed dishes until she calmed down—because she didn't want to lose control and risk damaging her relationship with her husband. In that moment, Gail realized that her ability to control her reactions was a muscle that she was flexing at home but not at work.

Once she saw that self-management was a tool she already had in her toolbox—and one she had been using successfully for years—she needed to decide how to bypass her automatic reactions and give herself time to think before responding to her employees. Gail and I eagerly brainstormed the office equivalent of "washing dishes"—so she could stop her boredom from devolving into belligerence. She decided to:

- Catch up on the reading in her newspaper basket

- Search the web for articles of interest to send to her staff, clients, or CEO

- Tune in to her iPod to decompress

- Take a walk

- Apply a top coat to her nails (which would keep her from "flaming" people over e-mail)

I encouraged Gail to post this list of options where she could see them readily—the equivalent of putting a bowl of fresh fruit on the kitchen counter for someone trying to commit to healthier eating. Gail typed up this list and made three copies: one for her computer keyboard, one for next to her phone, and one for her purse—in case she needed to take her new and improved act on the road.

Within a month of our initial coaching sessions, Gail had stopped losing her temper at work. Her staff definitely noticed the difference.

Gail's next step was to start communicating her preferences calmly and clearly to her staff. When I suggested to Gail that she let folks know how she felt about the hot-button issues she had identified, she responded with, "I'm sure they know, and if they *don't* know, I shouldn't have to tell them."

I asked Gail if she was more committed to being right or to making a change. As much as Gail really, really liked being right, she also really, really didn't want to lose her job. So Gail and I reviewed her list of "unacceptable" behaviors and boiled them down to two deal breakers: handing in incomplete work and disloyalty. As the boss, Gail was well within her rights to expect people to hand in high-quality work, and to expect them to have her back in public. She communicated this to her staff. Gail also acknowledged that she would demonstrate in her own behavior what she was demanding of others.

We identified two more behaviors—expecting praise for good rather than exceptional work and working too slowly—that were contrary to Gail's (strong) personal preferences but with which she might have to live at times. Gail admitted to her staff that she was not used to giving praise generously, nor did she feel particularly patient waiting for work to be completed. She also told her staff that she would aim to give a little more praise without going overboard and be more tolerant of others' production paces.

As for the final concern—staff leaving earlier than Gail would have liked—I suggested to Gail that she make the call based on whether or not the particular individual had completed his or her work for the day. The opportunity for a win-win here was tremendous—staff had to demonstrate their productivity (Gail's need) in exchange for being able to leave when they chose to (the staff's need). Gail agreed that anyone who wanted to leave at 5:00 p.m. could, as long as he or she got their work done.

Without question, Gail worked hard to make more effective and compassionate choices about communicating her needs and preferences to her team. Her efforts were rewarded by job security, improved staff morale and productivity, and the unparalleled feeling of victory that comes from battling destructive habits—and winning.

Good for Gail.

What about me? Was I willing to do the same for my home team? It looked like awfully hard work. And while I wasn't at risk of losing my job as a mother, I was risking my minions wishing they could fire me, or quit, or even worse—emulate my behavior. So, I applied the methodology I used with Gail to my own over-the-top reactions and have discovered that, while you'll rarely catch me washing dishes, I can take a moment, breathe deeply, and call a time-out for myself before communicating under stress.

Do I ever still "let it rip"? I do. But when I do, I have a team of coaches at home who just need to point at my left eyebrow to remind me of my commitment to thinking before I speak .

ACTION PLANNER

1. Identify your hot buttons.

When _____	I feel/do _____
Example: When my assistant submits my expenses late...	I feel frustrated and tell her she is irresponsible.

2. Identify your body's response to these hot buttons. Does your jaw clench? Does your heart pound? Do you sweat? List your physical signals here:

When I feel _____	Physically, it feels like/looks like
Example: When I feel frustrated...	My chest tightens and it's hard to breathe.

3. Even when we engage in behaviors that we know intellectually don't serve us in the long term, we do often reap some "hidden benefits" from them. For Gail, by blowing up in the moment, she reaped the benefit of having the issue over and done with, so she didn't have to think about it anymore. While it didn't serve her colleagues, it served her. Think about the benefits you're getting from losing your cool.

When I lose control of my temper, I secretly benefit by:

a. _____

b. _____

c. _____

4. Now think about the costs of letting it rip. Hurt feelings, loss of trust, instilling fear are all withdrawals you make from your "relationship bank account."

When I let it rip, the costs are:

a. _____

b. _____

c. _____

5. Brainstorm appropriate alternatives to the meltdown. From walking away to planning a vacation to creating a mantra, the options are limitless. What are all the appropriate things you could do to take a time out?

When I feel like I'm losing control, I could:

a. _____

b. _____

c. _____

d. _____

e. _____

6. Announce your plans to change your behavior publicly. Oh, yes—you just might have to involve other people— maybe even the very same people who push your buttons! Make sure that the other person has a chance to ask clarifying questions, like, "Do I have a ten-minute grace period for handing things in after the deadline?"

What will you say about what sets you off?

_____

_____

_____

What will you publicly commit to changing in your own behavior?

_____

_____

_____

What may you need someone to do differently in order for you to behave differently?

_____

_____

_____

7. **Bring others into the behavior change initiative.** Ask your staff or family what they would like to work on themselves. This suggestion comes from Marshall Goldsmith, who proposes in his book *What Got You Here Won't Get You There* that if everyone in your office (or home) is working on some behavior they'd like to change, they'll be more focused on what they need to do and less focused on finding fault with what you're working on. When everyone involved is focused on self-improvement, there's less energy for finger-pointing. Besides, once people start trying to change themselves, they'll realize that it takes effort—and may be more likely to cut you the slack you need to build momentum over time.

What behaviors would others like to work on? (This shouldn't come from you—even if you have a suggestion list a mile long. This needs to be self-generated and self-motivated.)

_____

_____

_____

8. **Ask for feedback about how well you are keeping your new commitments.** Former New York City mayor Ed Koch was well-known for stopping the city's notoriously blunt citizens in the street and asking, "How'm I doing?" Channel your inner Ed Koch and stop people in the middle of their day to ask, "How'm I doing?" as well as setting up formal times for feedback. And when you get feedback, Goldsmith notes, don't use that as an opportunity to express your own opinion. Just listen and thank the other person for being honest with you.

When will you ask, "How am I doing?"

_____

_____

_____

How can you be open to whatever feedback comes your way?

_____

_____

_____

9. Let your previous grievances go, and ask others to let theirs go as well. Holding on to historical slights and snubs keeps everyone in the past. This process is about moving forward.

What do you need to let go of?

_____

_____

_____

10. Do it. Take your time out and apply your redirection strategies rather than indulging in old, destructive habits. Will you mess up? Probably. Should you quit? Definitely not.

What can you tell yourself to stay on track?

_____

_____

_____

9

Two Ears, One Mouth

MY SON, JACOB, was furious with me. From his six-year-old perspective, I had just committed the ultimate offense—taking away his TV privileges for the night—for not listening to me. Choking on tears of frustration and moral indignation, he demanded that I absolutely, positively had to give him back television that night. Had to. Was going to. Now!

Calmly, I told him that I could hear how angry he was with me but that I was not going to change my mind. Hearing that, he lobbed the sharpest insult one could give a mom—or a professional coach: "You never listen to me!"

"Never listen?" I asked, wide-eyed and slack jawed. "Jacob, I listen to you all the time!"

"No you don't! You never do!"

"Jacob, I am listening to you right now."

"No, mom—you're *not* listening to me at all. I told you that you have to let me watch television! And you're not listening."

"I am listening. I heard you," I said, with a tranquil tone that I most certainly didn't feel. "And I said no."

"Then you didn't *listen to me,*" Jacob said.

I suddenly felt as if I was in the kind of bad dream where you find yourself in a foreign country, desperately seeking help, but nobody speaks English. What was going on here? What was the miscommunication? Since I was the grown-up here (both my height and the twenty-eight-year age difference clued me in), it was going to be up to me to figure this out.

"Jacob," I began. "What do you mean by 'listen to me'?"

My son looked me in the eye and said, "I mean what you mean when you say 'I want you to listen to me.' You mean, 'Do what I tell you to do.'"

Oh, yes. As in, "Jacob, listen to me: put your shoes in your closet now!" As in, "Jacob, I said no more cookies. Listen to me." As in, "It's lights out…Jacob, are you listening to me?" In each and every case, I was indeed using "listen to me" to mean "do it, and do it now."

Well, one thing was for certain—Jacob really, truly had been listening to me. How apropos that a six-year-old kid who worshipped

The tension between communication input and output is ages old

Batman would, in fact, have batlike hearing. But Jacob's ears picked up more than what I was saying. They heard what I was saying— deep down, where the meaning behind my words was inconsistent, insensitive, and sometimes insulting. Jacob was listening to me on a level that I hadn't matched in return. He was hearing me in a way I didn't hear myself, and, quite frankly, I didn't like what he—or I—was hearing.

Do you remember the first time you heard a recording of your own voice? Chances are, you remarked, "That's not what I sound like," and then looked around the room for other people to confirm this for you—that you didn't really sound so high-pitched or nasal, or have such a heavy accent. What happened? Your friends (or perhaps now, former friends) told you that yes, indeed, you did sound just like that. You probably felt disconcerted—how could you not hear yourself the way that other people did? Walter Matthau, as Oscar in the movie *The Odd Couple,* famously remarked when he was feeling ignored by his roommate, Felix, "I know I'm talking. I recognize my voice…."

Like Oscar, you may know you're talking, but unless you really make an effort to hear yourself the way other people do, you may not truly recognize the impact of your tone. But why is it so hard to listen—to ourselves and to others? The tension between communication input and output is ages old. God gave human beings two eyes, two nostrils, and two ears, but only one mouth. You don't have to be a rabbi, a doctor, or a mathematician to recognize that this two-to-one ratio indicates that we are supposed to be absorbing twice as much information from the world around us as we are to be producing new material. Nevertheless, the Torah tells us that when God blew a soul into Adam, he became a "speaking being," which immediately separated him—and eventually all of us—from the other animals on earth. So what makes us unique—our ability to speak—is also what trips us up when we want to talk far more than we want to listen. Author Fran Lebowitz accurately and succinctly summed it up in her book *Social Studies:* "The opposite of talking isn't listening. The opposite of talking is waiting." Waiting for what? For our turn to talk, of course!

Far too often, when we get (or take) that turn to talk, we're so committed to getting our own point of view across that we don't make the effort to consider others' perspectives, or to see how our message is landing. Sometimes it's because we want to make sure that our version of "the truth" is the one that comes out first, or loudest, or by itself. Sometimes, we are afraid to tell the truth, and so we create thinly veiled messages to hide what we really want to say. Still, there are other times we are afraid to hear the truth—and we don't want to create an opening where another person's competing version of the truth could come out. But what we fear tends to be worse than the reality. Sometimes it is completely the opposite. Susan Scott writes in her book *Fierce Conversations* that "companies and marriages derail because people don't say what they're really thinking," and that most of us really do want to hear the truth even if we may not like what we hear. In fact, Scott contends that "There is something within us that reponds deeply to people who level with us."

Of course, in order for us to say what we're really thinking, tell a difficult truth, or level with people in our work and our lives, we need to really hear ourselves the way other people do, to start listening to ourselves at a much deeper level. "Begin to overhear yourself avoid-

We need to really hear ourselves the way other people do

ing the topic, changing the subject, holding back, telling little lies (and big ones), being imprecise in your language, being uninterest-

ing even to yourself...[then] stop for a moment, take a deep breath, then come out from behind yourself in the conversation and make it real." Scott's friend Ed uses this handy and honest sentence when he hears himself saying something he doesn't mean: "What I just said isn't quite right. Let me see if I can get closer to what I really want to say." And then he finds a way to restate his thoughts until he hears himself say what he means.

According to a Jewish proverb, "No one is as deaf as one who will not listen." When I began working with my coaching client Julie, it was clear that she wasn't listening to herself or anyone else in her office.

As president of her publishing company, Julie was deservingly proud of her hard work, dedication, and success. However, her relationships with her employees were characterized by animosity and mistrust. As part of our 360° evaluation process, I spoke with the marketing director, Sandy, who said that she felt as if Julie showed no appreciation whatsoever for her contributions. In fact, Sandy told me that Julie often went around declaring that she herself was the president *and* marketing director.

I asked Julie to tell me about her relationship with Sandy. Julie told me that she felt frustrated by her because she was not performing to her standards. I asked Julie to tell me specifically how she communicated this feedback to Sandy, and she, herself, echoed Sandy's remarks—except that she described it as "joking" about filling all the roles herself.

I wasn't smiling.

"Julie, what part of this 'joke' do you think Sandy finds funny?"

"What do you mean?" Julie asked.

"I mean exactly what I asked you. What part of your joke do you think is funny to Sandy?"

I could see Julie shifting uncomfortably in her chair. "I'm not sure."

"Is it possible that she doesn't find it funny at all?"

"Yes," Julie admitted, "that's possible. But that's not really the point."

"So what is your point—really?"

"My point is that I'm frustrated with her performance, and I'm annoyed that I have to pick up the slack."

"Julie, I want to acknowledge your clarity and honesty in what you just said. You are frustrated with Sandy's performance, and you resent having to do parts of her job. Yes? Did I hear you correctly?"

"You heard me correctly. That's exactly it."

"So you are clear in your own mind about what's not working in Sandy's performance."

"Right. Sandy is slow to respond to requests from me, her colleagues, and clients. She delays us and holds up deadlines."

"Ok, that seems clear enough. So, now, tell me about your 'joke.' Why are you joking about this?"

Julie, now wincing at the word, plowed ahead into some serious insights. "I guess I had hoped that she would get the message without my actually having to deliver the message."

"Why didn't you want to deliver the message?"

Julie thought for a moment. "I didn't want to deliver the message because I didn't want her to get angry, or upset, or defensive—and now, of course, she's much more upset than if I had just told her directly and we had moved on."

"Yes, that sounds about right. And what other messages do you think Sandy is taking away from your 'joke'?"

"I think she hears me saying that she's not valued. That I don't think she can improve. That I'd be better off without her working here."

"And which of those is true?"

"None of them. I do value Sandy, I do think she can improve, and I don't want to replace her."

"How do you think she'd respond to that message, communicated directly?" I prompted.

"She'd be fine with it. She'd probably really appreciate it."

Julie scheduled a series of meetings to gather feedback from her management team. She stopped playing fast and loose with her language—saying one thing and meaning something far more serious. She started listening to herself and hearing her tone and messages the way that her staff did. Over several months, Sandy's responsiveness and performance improved, and Sandy felt like Julie was more appreciative of her contributions. Success.

We struggle with the gap between what we say and how we sound

US State Department spokesperson Robert McCloskey is said to have commented: "I know that you believe that you understood what you think I said, but I am not sure you realize that what you heard is not what I meant." If that's clear to you, then your work here is done. But for the rest of us, who struggle with the gap between what we say and how we sound, use the worksheet that follows.

ACTION PLANNER

1. Think about the common phrases, questions, or "jokes" that you use with your family, friends, co-workers, and direct reports to mask what you mean. For example:

You might say:
"Why don't we...?" (Making suggestions about weekend plans.)

When you sometimes really mean:
"This is what I want to do, and I expect you to agree to do it."

You might say:
"Oh, I see that you remembered to..." (Prepare agendas for the meeting, empty the dishwasher, copy accounting on an e-mail)

When you sometimes really mean:
"You should know to do this without my telling you."

You might say:
"I heard that movie got bad reviews." (Any movie I don't want to see.)

When you sometimes really mean:
"I don't want to see that. Let's go see my flick pick."

Write down what you say and what you actually mean.

At work:

When I say:	I really mean:

At home:

When I say:	I really mean:

2. Look for patterns in the lists above. Do you tend to give commands in the form of questions? Do you ask people to change a behavior by joking about it? What's hard for you to say or ask for directly?

I notice that I:

_____

_____

_____

3. Anticipate your roadblocks to communicating clearly. Are you worried about how someone will react? Not sure how to be "compassionate" while delivering direct feedback? Maybe you're hoping that someone will "take the hint" and do what you're asking—without your actually having to ask.

I am concerned that:

_____

_____

_____

4. Survey others. First, let your family or work colleagues know that you want to communicate more clearly and with more compassion, and that their feedback will help you to do that. You may need to promise both little kids and big kids that their contributions to this conversation will be taken seriously—and will not be held against them. (However, if you can't live by these rules, don't have these conversations.) Ask them these questions so that you can hear how others hear you:

- What do I say that drives you crazy?

- What do I say that you know means something else?

- What questions do I ask that sound more like suggestions or demands?

- What jokes do I make that have too much truth to be funny?

- What do I say to you that makes it clear that I don't hear myself the way you do?

5. Go deeper. For every phrase, question, or joke that has a hidden message, ask your friend, family member, or colleague how he or she would prefer to hear the message. For example, you might hear your husband ask you to make a direct request for him to clean out the refrigerator rather than have you say, "There seems to be penicillin growing back here!"

6. You may need to repeat and reinforce your commitment to using their feedback for good instead of evil.

Person	Old message	New message

7. Troubleshoot. If you sense that changing your approach might not yield the results you're looking for, ask what will do the trick. You may want to say, "I am committed to making my requests directly rather than as a joke. If I am not getting the result or response that I am looking for from you, how should I let you know that?"

8. Give it time. It probably took you a while to learn to craft your messages so creatively. It will take you a while to deconstruct them into clear and compassionate language. In addition, it may take your family, friends, and co-workers a while to appreciate your efforts and trust that they can give you clear and compassionate feedback, too.

What, This Old Thing?

In Praise of Praise

My son finally had me just where he wanted me: on the Long Island Rail Road, his plastic superhero collection in a bag, and forty-five minutes with nothing else to do.

Jacob pulled two caped and masked heroes out of the bag and immediately locked them in a death match. "You'll never get away with this!" "Oh, yeah? Try and stop me!" he dialogued, in a booming voice that no doubt could be heard from engine to caboose.

He looked up at me. "Come on, Mom! They need help! Fly in for a rescue!"

So I grabbed Batman from the baggie and held him aloft. "I'm flying in for a rescue!"

Jacob looked at me with disappointment.

"Mom. Batman doesn't fly."

Really? What's the cape for? Just a fashion statement? So I grabbed a green guy who looked familiar.

"Hulk flying in for a rescue!"

"Mom! That's not Hulk—it's Martian Manhunter. And he doesn't fly either." Jacob said, with thinly veiled exasperation.

I needed to get to the bottom of this before he told me that Aquaman was scared of the ocean.

"Jacob, I thought that all superheroes had superpowers—like flying."

"You don't need superpowers to be a superhero. You just need special talents."

Aha! Good to know. So I decided to see how he could apply that knowledge to real life—my life, to be specific.

"Jacob, if I were a superhero, who would I be?" I asked, priming him to reveal to me my many hard-won parenting skills and talents so that I could revel in them.

Jacob gave the question about three seconds of thought before answering:

"That's easy. You'd be 'The Oatmealer.'"

Making oatmeal—that's my special talent? "Jacob, do you know how easy it is to make oatmeal?" I inquired. "I mean, I just add water."

"And sometimes peanut butter," he reminded me.

"Okay, and sometimes peanut butter, but still..." I argued.

"It's my favorite breakfast and you make it the best. That's why you're 'The Oatmealer.'" Now can we please get back to *these* superheroes?"

In that moment, I decided to stop fighting and start focusing on the superpowers I had just learned that I held: turning rolled, steamed, cut, and precooked whole grains into a delectable, well-rounded, robust contribution to the most important meal of the day. For me, it's a no-brainer. For Jacob, it means a happy start to a busy day—something he really, truly values.

Whether you're cooking, campaigning, or doing crisis management, your contributions make you a superhero to someone—even if your special abilities feel run of the mill to you. But too often, two dynamics are at play that keep us from getting and giving the feedback we need (and yes, admittedly want) to feel good about what we do: we don't offer enough praise to others, and when we happen to find ourselves on the receiving end, we rebuff, reshape, or reject the praise we've been given.

When Dr. Gerald Graham, Professor of Management at Wichita State University, surveyed fifteen hundred employees across industries, he found the following:

1. 58 percent seldom if ever received praise from their manager
2. 76 percent seldom if ever received written thanks from their manager
3. 78 percent seldom if ever got a promotion based on performance
4. 81 percent seldom if ever received public praise
5. 92 percent seldom if ever participated in a meeting designed to build morale

When the same study asked participants to rank, in order, sixty-five potential motivators, guess which five emerged as the leaders? What people wanted and needed the most, they received the least!

So, what's getting in the way? Despite the fact that, according to its online article "5 Ways to Give Praise: Small Efforts with a Huge Return," the Center for Management and Organization Effectiveness reports, "most leaders agree that praise is important, that it leads to better morale, higher productivity, and builds a stronger relationship with employees," too many managers are too busy with their own work to prioritize giving positive feedback. In addition, when managers focus more on overcoming obstacles rather than cultivating and growing what's working well, they spend the vast majority of their time and attention on giving corrective rather than supportive feedback. Finally, when managers take their lead in tone, time, and temperament from above, they often find that they have no model for sharing positive feedback. In other words, they don't get it, and they don't know how to give it.

You don't need superpowers to be a superhero. You just need special talents

Proverbs 16:24 tells us, "Pleasant words are like honey, sweet to the soul and healing to the body." Not only do positive words make people feel better, they help people act better, too. Many of us know that if you want someone to repeat a specific behavior, you should acknowledge and praise the behavior specifically and immediately.

But there's a difference between offering praise ("Well done!") and offering praise plus encouragement ("Well done—and you deserve to feel proud of how hard you worked to get this accomplished"). The former feels good—like the sugar rush you get from downing a handful of M&M's®. The latter feels good *and* lasts—like eating an energy bar. They both taste sweet, but the energy bar will keep you satisfied longer, and you're less likely to need another fix immediately.

Managers often find that they have no model for sharing positive feedback

In his book, *Solving Discipline and Classroom Management Problems,* Charles H. Wolfgang offers examples that highlight the distinction between praise and encouragement:

Praise Statements

- "I (teacher) like what you have done."

- "Great job! What a smart person!"

- "You get a star (token, free time) for doing that."

- "I'm going to tell everyone how proud I am of you."

Encouragement Statements

- "You're trying harder."

- "You must be happy with...."

- "It must be a good feeling to know you're doing well."

- "You have every reason to be proud."

Praise is about expressing the speaker's values regarding what he or she likes and feels is important. Encouragement is about helping the other person take ownership of what he or she has accomplished, making it feel like an internal achievement in addition to the external admiration. Both praise and encouragement—preferably coupled together—deserve to be heard in every home, school, business, and community.

Do you want your husband to hand over the remote more often so you don't have to watch every single rerun of *Law and Order?* (And by "you" I mean "I.") Recognize it when he *does* relinquish control, praise him for it, offer encouraging words that reflect that you acknowledge the difficulty of his sacrifice, and over time, you may get the first pick—of first-run shows, no less—more often than not. Do you want your supervisor to process your expense reports more expeditiously? Give her a compliment and a thank-you each and every time, plus encouraging words that show that you see the effort she has made.

If it sounds too simple to you, you've got a point. Some methods of giving praise are more effective than others. In their book *Managing Up,* Michael and Deborah Singer Dobson share this acrostic to remind us how to give praise:

Personally

Regularly

Assertively

Immediately

Sincerely

Explicitly

Let's look at these one by one:

- **Personally, as in "Don't Delegate This One."** The Talmud tells us, "You may tell part of a person's praises to him or her directly." If you are the one who has witnessed or benefitted from what someone else has done, you should be the one to give the compliment. This is not something you should delegate to someone else. Furthermore, if you can share the feedback in person, do so. Now, I'm not suggesting that you hop a flight to Hong Kong to tell your regional sales manager what a great job he has done meeting his numbers and why he should feel proud to have accomplished this in a down economy. I am suggesting that if you can't do it in person, then get as close to "in person" as you can—Skype is better than a phone call, a phone call is better than e-mail, e-mail is better than a text message, and a text message is better than nothing, I guess. All that being said, a handwritten note is a wonderful way to share positive feedback that never goes out of style. Use it in addition to all of the above.

- **Regularly, aka "Once a Year Won't Cut It."** Of course, regularly doesn't mean "Wednesday is Praise Day." Nor does it mean all the time. In his article, "Trophy Kids: What Goes Around Comes Around!" Ira S. Wolfe writes,

  > The Millennial generation [those born after 1980] are truly "trophy kids." The Millennials were lavishly praised and often received trophies when they excelled, and sometimes when they didn't, to avoid damaging their self-esteem. They are also the newest employees entering the workforce. They will change the way organizations hire, manage and retain employees.

  With this in mind, it's important to know that giving praise regularly may mean giving it less often than what some people might want or expect if they've been raised on a daily diet of kudos and compliments. For folks who have learned how to achieve and excel without it, regular feedback may mean an increase in frequency. Regular praise means that it is a healthy and consistent part of your interpersonal relationships. The people in your work and life can and should come to expect it—which is not the same as being dependent upon it or feeling entitled to it.

- **Assertively—or "Take My Compliment... Please!"** If you've ever heard your colleague say "What, this old thing?" when you offered her praise on her terrific sales pitch to a big client, then you realized you had two choices: you could drop the matter altogether, or you could do your best to insist that she take the compliment. Of course, if you've ever said your own version of "What, this old thing?" then you've got mud on your hands.

We deserve to hear praise and encouragement—preferably together

Giving genuine praise feels good. When you reject the praise, you reject the person giving it. It's like handing back a present that someone has just given to you. That feels bad for everyone. Accepting praise is a positive sign of self-acceptance. Accepting praise establishes and develops interpersonal relationships because it requires an exchange of ideas and opinions. Accepting praise does not mean that you're done growing or improving—it simply means that you recognize that you've grown some already, and someone else noticed it, too.

Giving and accepting praise assertively is one of the hardest skills for people in the workplace—probably because we're so starved for it that, when it comes along, we don't know what to do with it, don't know what to say about it, and sometimes don't trust it. One of my favorite exercises to facilitate in feedback-starved organizations is called "Kisses of Appreciation" (the title, I admit, tends to alarm some HR managers.) In this surprisingly simple exercise, every participant gets three Hershey's Kisses and is asked to give two away to two different people in the room who have made a positive impact on the giver. In handing the kiss over, the giver is asked to tell the receiver specifically what he or she has done that has made a difference, and the recipients are instructed to receive the statement openly and warmly. The appropriate response for receiving feedback? "Thank you." Not "thank you, but..." or "Stop it already!" or "It's nothing, really." Just "thank you."

Where does the third kiss go? The third kiss is for the giver to keep, accompanied by a piece of self-praise and encouragement. For many participants, that last kiss is the hardest one to accept—but of course, it is ultimately the most important piece of chocolate (and praise) that they can receive that day.

- **Immediately, as in "Now or Never!"** In her book, *The Leader as a Mensch,* Bruna Martinuzzi writes: "Praise has a limited 'best before' date. Don't delay its expression or wait until performance review time—when you see something that is worthy of praising, do so promptly after the event." It's not better saved for a performance review or for your annual romantic vacation. When you give praise and encouragement in a prompt and timely manner, you are more likely to remember and convey the exact details of what worked well and why—and the more specifics that you can share, the more likely you are to have that positive behavior repeated. You've got something nice to say? Don't save it. Life is short, and so are our memories.

- **Sincerely...REALLY!**

  Consider this exchange from *Fiddler on the Roof:*

  Constable: You're an honest, decent person. Even though you are a Jew.

  Tevye: Oh... *thank* you, your honor. How often does a man get a compliment like that?

  Sadly, like Tevye, we give and get praise like that far too often: a compliment with a catch. Think about other praise-like phrases that take away more than they give:

  "Well done—for you." "Excellent job—so far." "That was terrific! Why didn't you do it like this before?" (Or, "Can't you do it this way all the time?")

  Do you see what gets in the way of sincerity? There's a string attached to every single one of these lines that, when given a gentle tug, begins to unravel the entire piece of positive feedback.

In order for your praise to feel sincere, it should be able to stand alone. Martinuzzi writes: "When you drop by an employee's office or cubicle to deliver the praise, don't follow that with a conversation about business matters or other projects. Deliver the praise and leave. Come back later for discussions on other matters. This gives the praise its moment of honor and heightens its value in the eyes of the recipient." When you attach the positive feedback to something else—a corrective comment, or even to mundane business matters, it makes the compliment feel like a condiment rather than the main course.

- **Explicitly, as in "Details, Details!"** Be as specific as you can with your feedback so that your message is crystal clear about exactly what worked for you and why. If you want to see explicit feedback in action, look no further than television's ever-growing lineup of cooking competitions. From *Top Chef* to *Iron Chef,* the culinary judges on these shows are well-armed with a critical palate, an eye for impressive plating, and some of the best explicit feedback skills I've seen in action.

Case in point: Battle—Chum Salmon. When Iron Chef Bobby Flay presented his dish, Fried Green Tomato with Smoked Chum Salmon, he received explicit praise from judge and esteemed food writer Jeffrey Steingarten: "I love the salmon on this dish because it's smoked, and that added a flavor that we haven't had before...and you didn't smoke it so long that it hardened its texture." The judge didn't say, "It's delicious," or "I love it," or "Wow, you really know your way around a salmon"—all of which are complimentary. What Judge Steingarten did was give Iron Chef Flay specific feedback about what worked, both in terms of the outcome (a new flavor) and the process (timing of the smoking).

Now, you may not need to go into as much detail as Judge Steingarten. It's probably enough to tell your assistant, "I appreciate how you fielded all my phone calls while I was out of the office for the past few days. I know that my customers felt well taken care of, and I like how you kept me in the loop with your e-mail status report at the end of each day." You probably don't need to add, "Your tone of voice was so soothing, and the font you chose for those e-mails really caught my eye." There's explicit, and then there's ridiculous. Be specific enough so that the recipient of your feedback knows exactly what you liked, why, and what the outcome was—and chances are, those behaviors will be repeated in the future.

In addition to being explicit with your praise, you also need to deliver feedback in the way in which the recipient is most likely to value it. My daughter, Sophie, prefers not to be center stage (which is lucky for her, since her mother and brother both love to hog the spotlight). When she was younger, she was reluctant to go up on the *bimah* with the other children to sing *Adon Olam* and *Ein Keloheinu* on Saturday mornings at synagogue. More often than not, she would sit with the adults, watching her brother and peers from the sidelines. Michael and I told her that she had a nice singing voice—but she didn't care. We assured her that she knew all the words—and she was unimpressed. It wasn't until the cantor told her that she was the *fastest* singer of the whole group that Sophie—a highly competitive athlete—was willing to take the stage.

Whether you're giving the recognition or receiving the kudos, remember that praise is a gift. Give it willingly, with an open heart, and without expectation of reciprocation. Accept it warmly, with a smile, and with a sincere "thank you." It's a gift that makes the present—and your presence in it—more positive.

ACTION PLANNER

1. What kind of praise feels most comfortable for me to give? To whom? What makes it feel comfortable?

_____

_____

_____

2. What kind of praise feels uncomfortable for me to give? To whom? What makes it feel uncomfortable?

_____

_____

_____

3. What kind of praise feels most comfortable for me to receive? From whom? What makes it feel comfortable?

_____

_____

_____

4. What kind of praise feels uncomfortable for me to receive? From whom? What makes it feel uncomfortable?

_____

_____

_____

_____

5. Whom do I know who receives praise with poise? What can I ask them about this that might help me?

_____

_____

_____

_____

6. What would I want someone to say when I praise them?

_____

_____

_____

_____

7. Who in my work or life could use some praise and encouragement from me?

_____

_____

_____

8. With whom will I start and what will I say?

_____

_____

_____

_____

11

Aren't You Leaving Soon?

WHILE MICHAEL packed our suitcases in preparation for our return trip home from five wet but wonderful vacation days in London, I gathered all of our used sheets and towels, stuffed them into a single pillowcase, and carried the sack into the kitchen where my friend and hostess Lisa was having breakfast. "Do you want me to wash these?" I asked her. "Just leave them," Lisa said. "I'll get to them later in the week."

"Really?" I asked, feeling guilty that I was giving her one more thing to do—especially after she, her husband, Jonathan, and their young son, Aidan, had shared their home, their food, and their toys with us for the better part of a week. When it came to fulfilling the mitzvah of *hachnasat orchim* (welcoming guests) our friends had done it with open hearts and an open home. They had taken time from work to be our tour guides, given us the keys to their apartment so we could come and go as we pleased, and even handed over their shiny new MacBook Pro so that we could e-mail our kids at sleepaway camp. Theodor Herzl, recognized as the father of modern political Zionism, once said, "Build your home in such a way that a stranger may feel happy in your midst." Lisa and Jonathan had done that—and more—and so it seemed like washing a few towels was the very least we could do.

"I can't just throw a load in?" I pressed.

"Really." Lisa gently insisted. "And by the way, Jonathan said that you guys were the perfect guests. And you were."

The perfect guests? Us? What an incredible compliment to receive, considering all of the things that could possibly have gone wrong—from minor irritations to major annoyances—and considering that I, in fact, have a shaky track record as a houseguest.

I recall my failure to hide my distaste when, as a child, a host would serve something that involved onions or mushrooms. "Yuck!" I would assert. "I'm not eating that. What else do you have?" My parents would apologize for my behavior while shooting me looks of horror and outrage. (I know this because those looks are part of my own parental repertoire today). As a young guest, I cared *I have a shaky* more about making sure my palate was pleased than *track record as* I did about the feelings of our hosts, who had put time *a houseguest* and effort into making a meal, or my parents, whose preference was not to be humiliated.

My tour of tactless guest behaviors continued into my early twenties, when I visited my older brother, Scott, his wife, Debra, and my niece, Shira, who was a baby at the time. As I sat on their sofa, watching their TV and eating their snacks, my brother came out of the bathroom, from which I had recently emerged post-shower, clutching a handful of long, beautiful, wavy strands of black hair. Hey—I knew that hair! That was my hair! As Scott handed me back my tresses, he calmly reminded me that my young niece used that tub for her baths, and that he would prefer she neither marinate in nor be strangled by the locks I had left behind. I had been so concerned with my own grooming that I hadn't thought about any potential health, safety, or aesthetic factors.

As an adult, I am still a work in progress. When I stay with my mom and stepdad, my mother is constantly scooping up—sunglasses from the sofa, magazines from the kitchen counter—and bringing them back to the guestroom where my stuff belongs. When I stay with my mother- and father-in-law at their summer house, I know for whom the bell tolls when they ask, "Who left all the lights on downstairs?" After fourteen years of this, I'm surprised they haven't started collecting a toll to help cover the electric bill.

I am also the mother of two works-in-progress. As houseguests, my children have been known to dismantle a thousand-piece Lego structure in two minutes that took hours for their cousin to build (sorry, Mark). They have sulked over meals that were prepared with the finest gourmet ingredients, hoping that some Kraft macaroni and cheese would magically appear in place of the wheat berry salad with scallions, pecans, and cranberries in a champagne mustard vinaigrette (our apologies, Connie). And as a family *in toto,* we have, ahem, stopped up a particular piece of plumbing across the North American continent (with our regrets, Oksana, Matthew, Wendy, Becky, Laurie, Tom, etc.).

Pirkei Avot (*The Ethics of the Fathers*) tells us to "Welcome everyone with joy." I must admit that we—I—have probably made it challenging for some to follow this guidance. From leaving organic and inorganic traces behind to kvetching about the menu, there was clearly room for growth. But apparently, on this recent trip, we were able to apply the wisdom of poet Arthur Guiterman who quipped: "Good manners may in seven words be found: forget yourself and think of those around."

These aren't just guidelines for stays in someone's home—these are solid principles for getting along with anyone, anywhere, on any turf. While the Talmud advises, "Whatever your host tells you, do," I recommend that you don't wait for your host to tell you to do something (or worse, wait until your host tells you to stop doing something). Below are three proactive steps to making everyone—host and guest—feel welcoming and welcomed.

1. **Overestimate your impact and underschedule your visit.**
   While you are quite used to—and perhaps even delighted by—your own schedule, daily habits, and bare minimum

requirements for daily life, your hosts probably have their own to contend with. While your home and environment are set up to meet your needs seamlessly, marrying your needs with those of another household can require a complex dance of compromise, contracting, and communication. I remember visiting a friend overnight who remarked in the morning, "Oh, the coffee maker has been broken for ages. I hope that's not a problem." And I assured her that it wasn't, while I choked back tears and quickly Googled the nearest Dunkin' Donuts. My need was my problem—and I needed to keep it between me and myself.

In her article, "How to Be a Good Houseguest," *Woman's Day* columnist Kimberly Fusaro advises you to remember that your host should not have to make things revolve around you. "Vegetarians don't need to swallow a hamburger with a smile, but they shouldn't expect their hostess and her family to stop eating meat. If you're staying with smokers, don't suggest they take it outside; and you can't ask pet owners to board their four-legged family members, even if they make you sneezy. Unless you have a potentially deadly allergy—which, by all means, you *should* alert your hostess to—it's up to you to adapt."

Even if you like to have a solid half hour in the shower, read the newspaper in a particular order, or arrange your toiletries on the counter by size, you should plan to make your needs less obvious. No matter how beloved you believe you are to someone else, the sheen on your positive impact is likely to be dulled a bit by the day-to-day impact of you just being you in someone else's space. Whether you are planning to sleep in someone's house or visit their office for a meeting, assume that you have a bigger ripple effect than you mean to and plan to stay for slightly less time than you think would be ideal.

2. **Adopt the Platinum Rule.** The Golden Rule tells us to treat others the way we would want to be treated. That's good— but not good enough for being an exceptional guest. Think about it: I don't mind people leaving a pair of shoes in the front hallway (as you can tell when you trip into my entrance). The Golden Rule would invite me to kick off my Keds in your foyer, too. The Platinum Rule one-ups the Golden Rule by suggesting that you treat others the way that *they* want to be treated. As a guest, you should go platinum in everything from housekeep- ing (make your bed even if you leave the sheets rakishly wrinkled and exposed at *Your host should not have to make things revolve around you* home) to tone of voice (keep your volume down in the wee hours even if you're a night owl or an early bird at home). This is also true of gift giving—whether what you are giving costs money or time. When we came to visit our friends in London, we packed a small token item for the grown-ups (and took them out for a gourmet dinner), but we strained the limits of our carry-on bags with presents for Aidan. We antici- pated that while any present would be appreciated, a selec- tion of toys specially chosen for their son would be what they would have wanted.

This was true for our gift of time as well. As parents, we knew that the best gift of our time would be to entertain Aidan. It was both a help and a pleasure to do so. If we had followed the Golden Rule, we might have given our friends some gourmet coffee, cheeses, and chocolates—things that Michael and I would love to get. But by following the Platinum Rule, we gave our friends what they wanted—their son entertained and, frankly, adored—and it was a win-win we never could have gotten with a box of Godiva. And it was even more delicious.

3. **Say and show your appreciation.** Bookend your stay with thank-yous—and include a few more for good measure. When you are invited to come, say thank you. When you are shown your accommodations—even if you are sharing the room with your great uncle's dusty *National Geographic* collection (the complete set)—say thank you. When you are fed, given towels, cleaned-up after, say thank you. When you are leaving, say thank you, and handwrite a note.

Assume that you have a bigger ripple effect than you mean to

And while saying thank you is good—*showing* your appreciation is just as important. If you see that the garbage bag is full, tie it up and take it out. If your host comes home from work tired, offer to prepare or order in dinner. If you are throwing in some laundry, offer to do a household load.

So let me thank you in advance for inviting me to come visit you. I accept. I promise to play with your kids and make the morning coffee—or the coffee run—and ignore your threadbare couch with the mismatched cushions. Everything is lovely. And thank you again for inviting me!

ACTION PLANNER

What does being a good host mean to you?

_____

_____

_____

_____

What does being a good guest mean to you?

_____

_____

_____

_____

Who were the top three guests you've ever hosted? Why?

First name of guest	What they did that you appreciated	What they didn't do that you appreciated	How you felt when you were with them

Who were the worst three guests you've ever hosted? Why?

First name of guest	What they did that bothered you	What they didn't do that bothered you	How you felt when you were with them

Reflecting on the previous chart, what themes do you notice?

_____

_____

_____

_____

_____

_____

When planning your next visit, how might you better "overestimate your impact"?

My needs or habits	How might these make an unintentional impact?	How can I soften this impact?
Example: I need quiet in the morning.	*My friends might feel like they need to tiptoe around me.*	*I can bring a white noise machine and let them know that I won't be able to hear them in the morning.*

In preparation for your next visit, how might you replace the Golden Rule with the Platinum Rule?

	What would I want?	What I think my host would want	What I will do
Gifts			
Personal space			
Communication			
Planning for our time together and apart			
Structuring our visit			
Use of facilities and supplies			
Special requests			
Flexibility			
Help around the house			
Involvement in day-to-day			
Activities			

12

Learn from Me, and Teach Me, Too:
How to Be Both Credible and Vulnerable

TWO MONTHS AFTER HURRICANE KATRINA devastated New Orleans, I was invited to Jackson, Mississippi, to give a keynote speech to the city's Jewish community about leadership in times of crisis. Jackson, not even two hundred miles from New Orleans, had almost doubled in size since the hurricane, with schools opening their classrooms to New Orleans's youngest refugees, homeowners offering their spare bedrooms to strangers, and social service institutions providing counseling, job and home placement, and loans to anyone who needed assistance. To me, the people of Jackson were true heroes for helping without question, and the people of New Orleans were equally as heroic for having left everything behind, accepting help, and starting over from scratch.

Moments before I was to begin my speech at the synagogue, I was taken by surprise when the rabbi gave me an *aliyah* (the honor of being called up to say a blessing over the Torah) on behalf of the community. I was puzzled. Why me, an outsider? I was surrounded by people who had made profound sacrifices; I had sacrificed nothing. I was in the midst of courageous citizens who had done extraordinary deeds on behalf of strangers; I had done nothing. The audience was filled with folks who had lost their homes, their jobs, and their possessions. This honor was being bestowed on an outsider, when it should have gone to one of the hundreds of people in the room who had done so much—or needed to ask for so much.

With these thoughts swirling in my head, I took my place at the podium, opened my mouth to speak—and broke down. Not a dainty tear or two slowly streaming down my cheek, barely streaking my makeup. This was loud, guttural sobbing. As a community member ran up to me with a pack of tissues, I tried

Not a dainty tear slowly streaming down my cheek, but loud, guttural sobbing

to calm myself down and plot my damage control. After all, I had now totally blown my confidence, my charisma, and my nose in front of two hundred people who had come to be inspired by me.

My moment of despair had caused me a serious setback, in my plans and to my professional persona. In one fell sob, I had undermined my credibility and my professionalism—and I still had an hour to fill. So I had to go on with the show, even though every molecule in my body wanted to crawl into the carpet.

Suddenly I realized that's what "Leadership in Times of Crisis" is about. What just happened needn't become a blow to my credibility. I had experienced a vulnerable, authentic moment that amplified my authority with a group of people who were undergoing their own crises. I now knew—and had demonstrated—how to keep going when the going gets tough.

And with that, I began my speech, not as an "outside expert," but as an insider who had just moments before had her own personal crisis in the public eye. I couldn't have planned it this way—and I also couldn't have asked for a warmer reception from the audience, who gave me a standing ovation before I even started my speech.

In our work lives, we know how important it is to be regarded as highly capable professionals who offer unique value to the team, to our bosses, and to the bottom line. Whether we're looking for a job or not, our resumes are chock-full of our impressive work credentials, volunteer experiences, and educational backgrounds—aimed to inform, and yes, impress. We want to demonstrate our credibility in whatever profession we're in. And that's a critical part of selling ourselves into a new job, or keeping the job that we have. Once we have the job, we don't stop our PR campaigns to show how smart and savvy we are. We keep at it, each and every day. And it gets exhausting trying to prove our expertise at every turn.

It's not just tiring—it actually can undermine our ability to make genuine connections to the people we're most concerned about impressing. We sell ourselves and our colleagues short when we fail to communicate that we're not just professional, we're impressionable as well. We're living and learning, too. We've had missteps and mistakes along the way. Strategically sharing those winding paths can help us connect with colleagues, clients, family, and friends on an even deeper level.

I have found that people are more attracted in work and in life to those folks who have mastered the balancing act between being credible and vulnerable. Clients, prospects, and colleagues certainly want us to know our stuff and have the credentials to back it up, but they also want to know that we have experienced our own doubts, fears, and growing pains. It's what makes us approachable, believable, and, yes, human.

The Japanese have a term for this: *wabi-sabi*. The principle of *wabi-sabi* asserts that there is greater value in something (or someone) with unique imperfections and flaws than in something polished to a perfect, unspoiled shine. In our family lives, we are usually willing to see our loved ones as worthy of respect, admiration, and adoration even when we are fully aware of their blemishes (and grandparents take this to the extreme—God love them). But many of us don't trust the people outside of our immediate circle of friends and family to see our shortcomings and still believe that we are capable, credible, and professional. We should.

In their book, *Click,* Ori Brafman and Rom Brafman share their years of research into why we "click" with certain people and in certain situations—and whether there is anything we can do to create more of these seemingly magical connections. What the brothers discovered is that there are certain behaviors that accelerate—and deepen—a relationship. One of those is vulnerability. They acknowl-

I had experienced edge how counterintuitive that seems: "Most of
a vulnerable, us think that when we make ourselves vulner-
authentic moment able we are putting ourselves in a susceptible, exposed, or subservient position. By revealing their inner fears and weaknesses, many feel they allow others to gain power or influence over them. But in terms of creating an instant connection, vulnerability and self-disclosure are, in fact, strengths. They accelerate our ability to connect with those around us."

I have put this theory to the test. In my role as a presentation skills coach, I used to lead my workshops and one-on-one sessions by starting with my experience—from my early victory as a high school public speaking national champion, to my membership in the elite National Speakers Association, to my experience coaching presenters in Fortune 100 companies, to my appointment as a visiting professor of executive communication at an international business school in China, yadda yadda yadda. Heady stuff. Great credentials. But it also widened the divide between where my clients were starting from as nervous, awkward presenters, and where I was as a seasoned professional. Could I possibly relate to them? Of course I could—but they would only know that if I started by sharing the story of my memorable meltdown in Jackson. Once I did that, I saw that my clients immediately connected to me at a different level—I had been where they were now, I had experienced the kind of humiliation that they feared the most, and I had lived to tell the tale. Authentic? For sure. Still credible? I might say even more so.

Leading with what's most human about myself—my flaws, my foibles, my faults—rather than what's superhuman about myself (able to deliver an hour-long speech without referring to a single note card!) has become a way of life for me. In fact, when I write or speak about my personal or professional experiences, I try to follow this guideline: "If there's going to be any fool in this story, it's going to be me." In other words, it's important for my listeners, learners, and readers to know that if I have a lesson to share, chances are, I learned it through living it. As the Israeli diplomat and policitician Abba Eban once remarked, "History teaches us that men and nations behave wisely only after they have exhausted all other alternatives." While I am neither a man nor a nation, I can totally relate: I behave more wisely not because I am smarter or more righteous, but because I have learned through living what doesn't work. And guess what? I'm still not done.

What about you? What if you stopped leading with your smarts and started reaching out with your heart?

In his book *Why Am I Afraid to Tell You Who I Am?* John Powell describes five levels of communication and makes the case for why we should practice shifting from the first three levels (which make up the bulk of our interpersonal chatter) to the latter two, where real intimacy begins. Powell considers the first three levels "transactional"—a simple exchange of information—whereas the last two levels are "connective"—a name that says it all.

Level 1: Small Talk, or "Phatic"—These are the social niceties of a typical networking event or cocktail party. Questions and statements such as, "How are you?" and "Lovely to see you again" are polite, and often necessary, but don't invite new information.

Level 2: "Factual"—No room for opinions and points of view here—just the facts, ma'am! At this level, you are simply sharing data. "Our staff meetings are every Tuesday at noon," "My triathlon is on

Sunday," or "Our company ships to the Far East." You're like a human Google, without the incomprehensible algorithm.

Level 3: "Evaluative"—This is where a basic exchange of opinions and ideas starts. There is greater risk—and greater reward—as you start to share thoughts, feelings, and points of view. These statements can range from the mundane, "I prefer my minivan to an SUV," to the more profound, "This is the most delicious brisket I have ever eaten." You begin to express yourself and, yes, hazard a disagreement or a turnoff, but, in general, this is a low-stakes gamble. This is where the transactional levels end and connective communication begins.

Level 4: "Gut Level"—Opinions and ideas give way to feelings and emotions. This level reveals our deeply personal perspective and unique sensitivities. Examples include, "Your friendship is so important to me," or, "When you come late, it feels like you don't care about my needs." Revealing, evocative, and not for cocktail parties—especially if you're on your third cocktail—these statements begin to build a bridge of trust and connection between people. You will both give and receive insight into what the other person thinks, feels, and values. Take it seriously. And while mutuality helps, it's not absolutely required. Sometimes, someone needs to take the first step into these deep waters. Sometimes, if it starts feeling too vulnerable, a brief return to a lower level of communication can provide you with some breathing space.

Level 5: "Peak"—This level reveals our innermost thoughts, fears, concerns, joys, and heartbreaks. Even in our most intimate relationships, we don't often venture here. Why? Because many of us haven't gone here with ourselves yet. And even if we're supremely self-aware, we aren't willing to risk turning our insides out for someone else to see—and judge. You'll recognize this level when you feel a deep sense of connection—"totally in tune"—with another person. Do you remember the heartfelt line in the movie *Jerry McGuire*, "You complete me"? Now that's a level 5 statement! Peak expression allows you to really, truly be seen—well beyond a list of credentials and accomplishments. The risks? That someone may really see you and reject you. Leading with this level of vulnerability is for your closest, most intimate relationships.

There is greater value in unique imperfections than a perfect, unspoiled shine

Whether you are ready to leap from level 3 to 4 in one relationship, or you're struggling to get out of level 1 in another, keep in mind that any progression is forward movement in bringing some authentic connection to your relationships. It's important to keep in mind that you can use this progression authentically—coming from a genuine place—and strategically—applied with intentionality—at the same time.

To give you an example of how effective this is, I often train volunteer and professional fund-raisers in the art and science of asking for money. And regardless of how much experience a solicitor has, and in spite of how deeply and passionately they believe in the cause, they often worry about how making the ask will be perceived by the donor or prospect. This anxiety can get in the way of solicitors asking with confidence—and can often prevent solicitors from asking at all—which directly impacts the organization's bottom line.

Some solicitors prefer to ask people whom they know well; others prefer to ask strangers, so that they don't overstep their bounds with friends and family. But before I am ready to teach them the key competencies of successful solicitation and give them opportunities to practice new skills or hone old ones, I know that I need to address the mental barriers first. In their study "Giving and Volunteering in the United States" researchers Virginia Ann Hodgkinson and Murray S. Weitzman found that a leading reason why donors give is because they are asked—and if asking becomes a major roadblock, so does giving. I open up the conversation by asking solicitors, "What are you most worried about?" when it comes to asking someone for money.

The range of responses includes:

- "I'm worried that my friends will think that I'm taking advantage of our relationship."

- "I'm worried that I won't be able to answer their questions."

- "I'm worried that people will look at me and start to think, 'Oh, it's the fund-raiser again!' and start to avoid me."

- "I'm worried that I don't know the person well enough to ask them for money."

- "I'm worried that they don't know enough about the organization in order for me to ask them for money."

No wonder so many nonprofits struggle to raise the funds they need! While some of it certainly may be about a shrinking donor base or reduced capacity to give, much of it may be about people's anxiety about asking. While I remind solicitors to tap into their own passion and commitment as part of the asking process, I recommend that they lead the solicitation conversation with their vulnerability—their care and concern for the relationship.

It could sound like:

"I'm excited to talk to you today about this organization, and I also want to make sure you don't feel like I'm taking advantage of our relationship. Our friendship is very important to me. So if it starts to feel that way to you, would you please let me know?"

Or it could sound like this:

"I have been involved with this organization for the last five years— and I'm still learning about everything they do and all of the ways that they help. So I might not be able to answer all of your questions today, but I do promise to listen and get back to you with any information you'd like. Would that be okay with you?"

It's not leading with an apology. It's not leading with an escape.

It's leading with an intentional sharing of interest in the relationship, the conversation, and, of course, the organization or cause. It sets the tone for an exchange that may explore four out of five communication levels—all of which might be appropriate for a deep discussion of interests, values, and commitment. What the vulnerable lead-in also does is it allows the fund-raiser to model honesty, integrity, and openness—three elements that one would hope that a prospect or donor would bring to the conversation. It also names the elephant in the room so that both parties can address it, move past it, and relax.

Managing to be both professional and vulnerable is a balancing act, for sure. We always need to be aware of how much of ourselves we share with others, and ensure that what we reveal doesn't expose something that will harm us—or others—in the *Lead with what's* long run. We also don't want to undermine our *most human* hard-won expertise and our credentials by down- *about yourself* playing what we know and what we've accomplished. But if you find that you are selling yourself to your colleagues and clients solely by relying on how smart you are or what you've achieved, you are selling yourself short. By adding in a healthy dose of the tricky, thorny, and, yes, sometimes funny ways in which you got so smart or achieved so much, you'll find that you can make a connection that is based on mutual respect, connection, and the truth.

ACTION PLANNER

In what relationships do you tend to reinforce your credentials—what you know, how experienced you are, how successful you've been—the most?

_____

_____

_____

_____

_____

In what relationships are you mostly communicating at the transactional levels (1-3) rather than the connective levels (4,5)?

_____

_____

_____

_____

How does keeping communication at the transactional levels serve you? What do you gain from it?

_____

_____

_____

_____

How could becoming more vulnerable—making a
connection, sharing feelings and concerns, exchanging
core values—serve you in these relationships?

_____

_____

_____

_____

_____

What concerns you about sharing your vulnerabilities?
What could it cost you?

_____

_____

_____

_____

_____

What assumptions about your concerns and the possible
costs are you making here?

_____

_____

_____

_____

_____

What if—like the solicitors-in-training—you shared those concerns with others? What's the best that could happen?

_____

_____

_____

_____

What will you try? How will you know if it was successful?

_____

_____

_____

_____

Use the space below to list some possible connective conversation starters (Level 4) to try with someone at work or in your personal life:

For example:

"As my manager, you have helped me learn what it means to give and get constructive feedback—and I really appreciate that."

"When you make plans without asking me first, it feels to me like you don't care about my input. I feel unimportant—and that hurts me."

_____

_____

_____

_____

13

In God We Trust:
All Others...Not So Much

DURING ONE OF our many girl talks, on topics ranging from boys to basketball, Sophie gave me a very special compliment: "Thank you for always telling me the truth."

I can't take credit for "always," but I do have a pretty good track record for being honest. I recently received accolades for my home-made ice-cream sandwiches. When the recipe was wheedled out of me, I had to admit that the cookies were baked from a mix, and the ice cream was made by Ben & Jerry's. Admiration for the funky leopard-print wallpaper in the living room must be conceded to the previous homeowner. And any commendations I get for appearing to balance work and life belong to my husband, Michael, and the team of grand-parents, aunts, uncles, and babysitters who make it all possible.

But this compliment I knew I deserved. I do tell Sophie the truth. Maybe not the whole truth (until I believe she's ready for it), but I don't skirt the tough topics. I'd rather she get accurate information from me than from a friend, the television, or the Internet. If I want Sophie to have faith in me—especially as we get ready to enter those teen years—I know that truth is the ticket.

That being said, I must admit that I was taken aback by how this conversation continued. Directly after offering me such high praise for my honesty, she followed with this comment: "That's why I trust you second-best in the whole world."

My mind was scrambling. Who was she putting above me? Who had earned more trust than I? Was it Grandma? Michael? God? I didn't know which of these would bother me the most, but I was determined to find out.

"So," I asked, my heart pounding with anticipation, "Who do you trust the most?"

Sophie looked at me as if I had just asked her to remind me of the sum of one plus one. "Myself, of course!"

Well, who was I to try to compete with that? Sophie trusted herself the most, which contributed to an unusual sense of self-confidence that showed up in her schoolwork, her basketball playing, and even her sense of personal style that has had her shop-

Thank you for always telling me the truth

ping in the boys' department since she was three. I was happy to be second banana for once. Sophie was living out the wisdom of Golda Meir, who once said, "Trust yourself. Create the kind of self that you will be happy to live with all your life." And my wish for Sophie is that her self-trust will indeed last long into the future.

I realize that not everyone is like Sophie. Many of us struggle to trust ourselves and others, at work and in life. Maybe we're unsure of our supervisor's motives behind a decision that seems to favor one employee over another (especially when we are the other), or we can't count on our best friend to show up for the movies at the agreed-upon time. Perhaps you don't have faith in your ability to avoid the bread basket at dinner, or you're not convinced that you will stick to your new exercise routine. In each of these cases, trust is fleeting, which can lead to difficult relationships and diminishing self-confidence.

Trust can be broken down into four separate elements, according to Charles Feltman, author of *The Thin Book of Trust*. The four elements are:

1. **Sincerity:** You say what you mean and you mean what you say. You are honest, believable, and can be taken seriously. Your opinions are based in evidence and careful thought. Your words and actions match each other.

2. **Reliability:** You keep your promises and meet your commitments.

3. **Competence:** You have the knowledge, skills, and abilities to do your tasks or job (and other people believe that you do, too).

4. **Care:** You have goodwill toward others, keeping others' interests in mind when you make decisions or take actions.

When one or more of these elements is missing, trust goes out the window. Feltman writes, "The disaster of distrust in the workplace is that the strategies people use to protect themselves inevitably get in the way of their ability to effectively work with others." I would add that the disaster of distrust toward ourselves is the growing need to solicit others' input, opinions, and advice for our own decisions, as well as our shrinking willingness to take risks—large or small. When that occurs, we live according to what others want for us. And as we find ourselves repeatedly aligning our choices with others' opinions, our own levels of self-trust erode even further.

One of my clients, Sharon, had had a long-standing, positive relationship with her supervisor and was well thought of in her company until trust started eroding right before her eyes. Sharon had been working at this midsize financial services firm for sixteen years and came to me for coaching when she had her first poor performance review in her long history with the company. "I don't understand," Sharon commented. "All of a sudden, I'm not meeting my boss's expectations? Out of nowhere?" Sharon was questioning the sincerity of the review—one of the four factors of trust.

I asked her to explore the idea that these changes came "out of nowhere." "What's happening over there? Is it business as usual?"

Sharon shared that about six months ago her company had been approached by a larger firm wanting to merge. "Our leadership announced that a possible merger *could* be happening. And that was the last I heard of it— that was months ago."

I'm scared that I'm being pushed out of the company

"And now, seemingly 'out of nowhere,' you have a poor performance review."

"Right." Sharon said. "But it can't be out of nowhere. There must be something going on. Maybe it's about the merger. Who knows?"

"It seems like you need more information, doesn't it? To know if this is out of nowhere—or out of somewhere."

"Yeah, I guess so. But I'm scared to find out," Sharon admitted.

"What are you scared of?"

"I'm scared that I'm being pushed out. Maybe I'm a redundancy if they're merging. Maybe I'm overpaid. Maybe they want someone younger. Maybe…"

"That's a lot of maybes," I remarked.

"But I don't trust them to really tell me the truth," Sharon said, sounding defeated.

"Why is that?"

"Because this bad performance review was so out of left field that I don't feel like I know my boss anymore. And if I don't know her, or what's motivating her, I can't trust her." Sharon was now concerned about the lack of reliability and care she was being shown, in addition to her doubts about sincerity.

"I can understand how you would feel that way if this review was inconsistent with all the other messages you were getting."

"Exactly!"

"And I think that's exactly the right place to start with your boss.

Highlight the fact that this review was inconsistent and that you're curious about it."

"Curious, not furious?" Sharon laughed.

I laughed with her. "You can absolutely feel furious. But I would lead with curious so that you don't put your boss on the defensive."

"Good idea." Sharon said.

Sharon decided that she would schedule a time to sit down with her boss, Eve, to discuss the performance review's inconsistency with previous feedback. When the time came to meet, Sharon started the conversation by stating her positive intention: to understand what was behind the evaluation so that, if needed, she could work to improve the behaviors or learn the skills that were needed. She was surprised to see Eve caught off guard and then remorseful. Eve told her that the company was likely going through with the merger and that the new company's performance evaluation standards were much more stringent. In an attempt to align the two companies' performance metrics, the leadership had put pressure on the management team to "be brutal" with this year's performance evaluations. Eve had wanted to insure her own future in the new organization, so she had thrown Sharon under the bus, and she was sorry.

Sharon appreciated the apology, but she also wanted more information. "What will this merger mean for us—for me?" she asked. Eve confessed that she didn't really know but that the rumor mill was churning with buzz that Sharon was indeed the redundancy she had feared. Two months later, Sharon was let go.

When Sharon and I spoke about how her long-term position had come to a less-than-happy ending, I was struck with how upbeat she was.

"I'm really proud of myself," Sharon said.

"About what specifically?"

"I'm proud of the fact that I really trusted myself. I knew that I hadn't earned such a poor review. I knew somehow that if I got a review like that one, there was something else going on. I trusted my own abilities and skill sets—and history, quite frankly—enough to know that this

Trust yourself enough to believe in your capabilities

wasn't a reflection of me. It was a reflection of something else—I just didn't know what."

"So, you trusted yourself enough to believe in your capabilities despite feedback that said otherwise."

"Totally." Sharon said with certainty. "You know the old dating excuse, "It isn't you, it's me?"

"I sure do!" I smiled.

"Well, in this case, I knew that it wasn't me. It was them!"

"Good for you!" I applauded her. "And you trusted yourself to have a hard conversation, even though you were scared of what you might hear," I added.

"Thank you," Sharon said. "And I trusted myself to handle whatever was going to happen—for better or for worse."

"And so what's next?"

"Next, I trust myself to find a new job in a place that values what I bring to the table," Sharon said, sounding emboldened.

"And a job working with people you trust?"

"Oh, yes. That, too."

I knew that when Sharon went for her job interviews, she would be interviewing her interviewers as well, assessing how trustworthy the people and the organization seemed to be. While there were no guarantees for Sharon—or for any of us—she had learned how important sincerity, reliability, competence, and care are for her professional and personal well-being.

When it comes to my relationship with my beloved morning cup of coffee, I am a fan of those pink packets of "the fake stuff." But when it comes to my relationships with my clients, my family, my friends, and myself, I won't settle for anything less than authenticity, believability, truth—in other words, trust. How about you?

ACTION PLANNER

What's your definition of "trust"? How does your definition relate to the four features of trust: sincerity, reliability, competence, and care?

_____

_____

_____

_____

How has your definition of trust served you?

_____

_____

_____

_____

Has it cost you anything or any relationships?

_____

_____

_____

_____

Who models trust for you in your personal or professional life? What are the observable behaviors you associate with and value most about trust?

_____

_____

_____

_____

_____

For whom do you model trust in your personal or professional life? With what behaviors?

_____

_____

_____

_____

_____

How could you get more feedback about how trustworthy you are? Whom could you ask?

_____

_____

_____

_____

_____

_____

Whom would you be least likely to ask about your trust-worthiness? What makes them the "least likely" person? (Hint: there has probably been a breach in at least one of the four features of trust.)

_____

_____

_____

_____

Use the table below to examine trust in your personal and professional relationships. Where is there room to improve?

Person	My perception of sincerity	My perception of reliability	My perception of competence	My perception of care
My supervisor _____	☐ Poor ☐ Moderate ☐ Excellent	☐ Poor ☐ Moderate ☐ Excellent	☐ Poor ☐ Moderate ☐ Excellent	☐ Poor ☐ Moderate ☐ Excellent
My colleague _____	☐ Poor ☐ Moderate ☐ Excellent	☐ Poor ☐ Moderate ☐ Excellent	☐ Poor ☐ Moderate ☐ Excellent	☐ Poor ☐ Moderate ☐ Excellent
My colleague _____	☐ Poor ☐ Moderate ☐ Excellent	☐ Poor ☐ Moderate ☐ Excellent	☐ Poor ☐ Moderate ☐ Excellent	☐ Poor ☐ Moderate ☐ Excellent
My colleague _____	☐ Poor ☐ Moderate ☐ Excellent	☐ Poor ☐ Moderate ☐ Excellent	☐ Poor ☐ Moderate ☐ Excellent	☐ Poor ☐ Moderate ☐ Excellent
My spouse/partner _____	☐ Poor ☐ Moderate ☐ Excellent	☐ Poor ☐ Moderate ☐ Excellent	☐ Poor ☐ Moderate ☐ Excellent	☐ Poor ☐ Moderate ☐ Excellent

My friend _____	☐ Poor ☐ Moderate ☐ Excellent	☐ Poor ☐ Moderate ☐ Excellent	☐ Poor ☐ Moderate ☐ Excellent	☐ Poor ☐ Moderate ☐ Excellent
My friend _____	☐ Poor ☐ Moderate ☐ Excellent	☐ Poor ☐ Moderate ☐ Excellent	☐ Poor ☐ Moderate ☐ Excellent	☐ Poor ☐ Moderate ☐ Excellent
My friend _____	☐ Poor ☐ Moderate ☐ Excellent	☐ Poor ☐ Moderate ☐ Excellent	☐ Poor ☐ Moderate ☐ Excellent	☐ Poor ☐ Moderate ☐ Excellent
My mother _____	☐ Poor ☐ Moderate ☐ Excellent	☐ Poor ☐ Moderate ☐ Excellent	☐ Poor ☐ Moderate ☐ Excellent	☐ Poor ☐ Moderate ☐ Excellent
My father _____	☐ Poor ☐ Moderate ☐ Excellent	☐ Poor ☐ Moderate ☐ Excellent	☐ Poor ☐ Moderate ☐ Excellent	☐ Poor ☐ Moderate ☐ Excellent
My sibling _____	☐ Poor ☐ Moderate ☐ Excellent	☐ Poor ☐ Moderate ☐ Excellent	☐ Poor ☐ Moderate ☐ Excellent	☐ Poor ☐ Moderate ☐ Excellent
My sibling _____	☐ Poor ☐ Moderate ☐ Excellent	☐ Poor ☐ Moderate ☐ Excellent	☐ Poor ☐ Moderate ☐ Excellent	☐ Poor ☐ Moderate ☐ Excellent
My child _____	☐ Poor ☐ Moderate ☐ Excellent	☐ Poor ☐ Moderate ☐ Excellent	☐ Poor ☐ Moderate ☐ Excellent	☐ Poor ☐ Moderate ☐ Excellent
My child _____	☐ Poor ☐ Moderate ☐ Excellent	☐ Poor ☐ Moderate ☐ Excellent	☐ Poor ☐ Moderate ☐ Excellent	☐ Poor ☐ Moderate ☐ Excellent
Myself _____	☐ Poor ☐ Moderate ☐ Excellent	☐ Poor ☐ Moderate ☐ Excellent	☐ Poor ☐ Moderate ☐ Excellent	☐ Poor ☐ Moderate ☐ Excellent

Review the previous table. For those relationships where you rated most elements as "Excellent," how can you share your appreciation for the trusting relationships you have with those people?

_____

_____

_____

For those relationships where you rated one or more elements as "Moderate" or "Poor," how can you share your feedback with those people in a way that will build trust in both directions?

_____

_____

_____

How do you think the people that you assessed would assess you? Go back and make some notes on your table. Then ask yourself, "What can I do to improve trust from their perspective?"

_____

_____

_____

How well do you trust yourself? Where is there room to improve?

_____

_____

_____

PART 3

Get Things Done

Dropping the Latke:
The Perfectionist's Dilemma

"THE GRAND THING about cooking is that you can eat your mistakes."—Julia Child.

In his *New York Times Magazine* article, "Out of the Kitchen, Onto the Couch," Michael Pollan highlights the famous episode in which Julia Child shows her viewers how to handle a larger-than-life latke (potato pancake), as well as how to handle themselves when life doesn't go as planned.

As Julia sautés a giant mound of mashed potatoes, cream, and butter, she prepares herself and her audience for her plating prowess.

"When you flip anything," Julia declares to the viewers, "you just have to have the courage of your convictions." As she gives the latke a flip, half of the dish catches the edge of the pan and falls back onto the stovetop.

What does Julia do? She scoops up the mess and tries to put the pancake back together. Turning to her audience, she confesses her culinary mistake: "When I flipped it, I didn't have the courage to do it the way I should have." Her next comment, however, goes beyond cooking technique—it reflects an attitude toward life. Don't let the mistake paralyze you, she tells her viewers. After all, "You can always pick it up...Who is going to see?"

Fortunately, when we make our mistakes, they are not usually broadcast on television to millions of viewers. But too many of us treat our errors as marks on our permanent record—to be carried with us throughout eternity. In a time when the ever-changing world requires us to be resilient and adaptable, our perfectionism keeps us rigid, locked into unrealistic expectations and counterproductive behavior. As astronomer Carl Sagan once

Don't let a mistake paralyze you

commented, "The universe is not required to be in perfect harmony with human ambition." Just because we want something to turn out according to our standards (as reasonable or unreasonable as they may be) doesn't mean it won't turn out some other way.

Over a decade ago, I was committed to making my newborn twins' homecoming perfect. Having been on bed rest for the three months leading up to their birth, I had plenty of time to plan for their arrival home. But four days after Jacob and Sophie were born, Michael and I were permitted to bring our robust seven-pound son home while our daughter, at just four pounds, had to stay in the NICU. With one baby in arms and one left behind, our return home was far from perfect. I would quickly learn, however, when perfection would be critical—and when good enough was good enough.

On our first night home with Jacob, we swaddled him in blankets to protect him against the bitter January draft and put him down in his bassinet. Michael and I fell into bed, clasped each other's hands in fortitude against whatever the night might bring, and fell into a deep sleep.

Less than an hour into our slumber, Jacob awoke, sniffling and coughing. Like any new parent, I leapt from bed to check on him. He looked up at me with his big hazel eyes, as if he were begging me for relief from his stuffed nose. Wanting Michael to get his rest, I lifted Jacob from his bassinet and carried him into the bathroom. I blasted the hot water from the shower and cradled our baby in my arms as steam filled the room. As the two of us grew damp, it became clear that the steam treatment wasn't good enough. He needed medicine.

I used my free arm to dig around in the freshly stocked basket of baby medicine we had prepared. Baby Tylenol—check. Baby Advil—check. Baby Butt Paste—check. Where was the Baby saline nose spray? Nowhere. Our preparations hadn't been good enough, and Jacob's congestion was going from bad to worse. I would have to take extreme measures: I would have to wake up Michael.

"Honey…Michael…MICHAEL!!!!" I nudged my husband awake with increasing urgency. "Jacob is congested, and we don't have saline nose drops. I need you to go out and get some now."

Michael rolled over, shielding his eyes with his forearm from an imaginary ray of light.

"Just use the contact lens solution," he said groggily. "Saline is saline; it's good enough."

Contact lens solution? Up our new baby's nose? Was he out of his mind?

Eye drops were not nose drops. Good enough was not good enough. This called for perfect.

"Michael, if we damage this baby, they will not let us bring the second baby home. Now get up and get the nose drops!"

He did, of course. Jacob survived the sniffles, and four days later, we brought Sophie home. The timing was perfect: She came home the morning of her brother's *bris* (Jewish ritual circumcision) and her own baby naming.

Over the past decade, while dealing with diaper rash, tantrums, and struggles with science fair projects, I have often asked myself, "Does this need to be perfect, or is good enough good enough?" As a coach, I regularly ask my clients this question. In fact, I find that many clients come to coaching as self-diagnosed procrastinators, putting off important projects and ambitions for weeks, months, or even years. In many cases, we discover that procrastination is masking perfectionism. When they don't know how to do it perfectly, they can't get started, they can't get finished, or both. Sound familiar?

It's an old refrain—really, really old. According to *Pirkei Avot,* "You are not obligated to complete the work, but neither are you free to desist from it."

"Complete the work" can mean many things, from "get it done now," to "get it done right," to "get it done inexpensively." For many of us, we're not finished until it's flawless, and even then, we're still looking for our "Sacred C.O.W.S."—the Couldas, Oughtas, Wouldas, and Shouldas. What does this relentless pursuit of perfection cost us?

Money, time, energy, relationships, and attention diverted away from those things that really need to be just right because the costs are too high to settle for good enough. Like what? Like when your emotional, physical, or financial safety and security are on the line.

Many of us treat our errors as marks on our permanent record

Alistair Ostell, a lecturer in psychology at the University of Bradford Management Centre in England, has identified the perfectionist's mindset: "absolutist thinking." This black-or-white approach leads to emotional distress—often anger—when we are confronted by situations that do not align with our demands of what should happen, even when those demands are self-imposed.

In her *Psychology Today* article, "The Cost of Perfection," writer Amy Wilson describes how absolutist thinkers "get upset if things don't go their way, which impedes their problem-solving and coping skills… This may translate into health complications such as insomnia, heart palpitations, chronic fatigue and high blood pressure." Furthermore, when we get angry, the resulting secretion of stress hormones can suppress our immune systems, making us more prone to infection. And if you're a perfectionist, you absolutely can't afford to get sick— because then you might have to lower your expectations and settle for less-than-perfect—which could really make you sick, right?

Wrong. Replacing the entrenched belief that flawlessness is the goal with the novel belief that good enough can be good enough can be painful, difficult, and even stressful—but it won't make you sick like striving endlessly for perfection can.

Monica Ramirez Basco, author of *Never Good Enough,* says that "each of us has a set of central beliefs about ourselves, other people and the world in general and about the future. We use these beliefs or schemas to interpret the experiences in our life, and they strongly influence our emotional reactions. Schemas can also have influence on our choice of actions."

If you're a perfectionist, do you think:

- If my presentation is perfect, then I will get more respect from my boss.

- If my appearance is perfect, then I will find a romantic partner.

- If my parenting is perfect, then my children will be happy, healthy, responsible citizens.

And of course, perfectionists are exceptional catastrophizers, so you may recognize some of these beliefs as well:

- If I make a mistake in my work, then I will get fired…and become poor…and have to move out of my house and live with my parents.

- If I make a mistake on my diet, then I will quit my diet…and gain a ton of weight…and be unattractive and unlovable… and die alone.

- If I make a mistake with my kids, then they will screw up in school…and get kicked out of school…and never be able to get a job…and will be dependent on me forever.

Our black-or-white, all-or-nothing, if-then hyperbolic thinking keeps us locked in this pattern.

My client, Leah, needed to be liberated from a thought pattern that kept her chained to perfectionism. Leah had been working in a small digital advertising agency for the past three years, following twenty years of work in more traditional advertising agencies. She was a highly regarded, seasoned pro, who prided herself on her ability to achieve exceptional results for her clients and for her company. During her three years at her firm, she had made herself an invaluable part of her team, and the agency overall. Leah had helped her agency win several accounts in two lucrative industries, pharmaceuticals and telecommunication, bringing in several million dollars of new business. In addition, three high-end clients had followed Leah from her old advertising firm to her new company, bringing Leah and her agency positive publicity in their trade publications, as well as a boost in their overall reputation. Leah's attention to detail, her powerful interpersonal relationships, her talent, her tenacity, and her hard work had recently opened a new door for her: her boss wanted her to take over as the COO of the agency—a newly created position. Leah was delighted, and despite the fact that she had never worked at the C-level before, she readily accepted the job. This was to be her dream job—the culmination of almost twenty-five years of work within her industry.

Two months into her position, Leah called me for coaching. She was overworked and overwhelmed, short-staffed and underfunded. She was falling further and further behind in accomplishing the goals set for her new high-level position—and hadn't discussed any of this with the CEO, her boss. And now she was panicked. She wasn't sleeping well, she had stopped exercising, and she was having stomachaches on a daily basis.

As I listened to Leah describe her work history—a long account of success—I heard the clues that led me to think she might be struggling with perfectionism. Leah described her fear of making mistakes, her concern about embarrassing herself, and her belief that there is a right way and wrong way of doing things. She also explained that she felt good about herself only when she accomplished exactly what she set out to do, like winning new business for her agency or bringing her old clients with her into her new agency. When she fell short of her expectations for herself, she felt anxious, sad, and a degree of self-loathing, like when two clients whom she expected to follow her to the new agency stayed with her previous firm. She felt her colleagues admired her for her professional achievements, rather than liking her for who she was as a person, *Does this need to be perfect, or is good enough good enough?* separate and apart from her wins. She feared that if her colleagues, direct reports, or supervisors ever saw the cracks in her facade— her self-doubt, her anxiety, her worries about the job with which she had been tasked—they would stop respecting her personally and professionally.

Leah was struggling with perfectionism. And her quest to find the one and only right way to do a job that she was still growing into was making her sick.

I asked Leah to talk though some of her "if-then" thinking: "If I make a mistake, everyone will think that I didn't deserve this promotion, and nobody will respect me anymore, and then I'll lose my job, and my reputation will suffer, and I'll never find work in this industry again. That will be it for me."

With thinking like that, no wonder Leah was scared. In her mind, she was one uncrossed *t* or undotted *i* away from no longer being able to make her living in the industry she adored, and the only industry she had ever worked in. The threat felt real—and imminent—to her. To deal with black-or-white perfectionistic thinking like Leah's, we were going to have to search for an example of a real debacle that she had experienced—and survived—without her having lost everything that she feared.

"Leah," I began gently. "Tell me about a time that you suffered a major setback at work or in your personal life." Notice I didn't ask her whether or not she had—I assumed that she, like the rest of us, had experienced a big slip-up, a giant omission, or a serious inaccuracy, and I didn't want to offer her an out.

Leah was quiet. After a while, she told me about a client presentation she had made early in her career. Her agency at the time was creating campaigns for two competing household products (picture Ajax and Comet—I promise those aren't the real ones), and she inadvertently researched Ajax, put together a pitch for Ajax—and delivered the pitch to Comet.

This was no small mistake—and I acknowledged how difficult it must have been for Leah to share that with me. She recalled the feeling of humiliation when she realized her mistake, her supervisor dressing her down, and the commitment she made to herself that she would never, ever make a mistake like that again.

"And what else did you learn from that mistake?" I asked.

"What do you mean?"

"I mean: What did you learn from that mistake that still serves you today?"

"Well," Leah began. "I learned to color code my files, have an assistant double-check the research, and…"

"Yes?" I prompted.

"And I learned that I didn't die. I didn't even get fired. I just felt horrible."

Leah admitted to her boss that afternoon that although she had been dancing as fast as she could, she couldn't keep up any longer. To Leah's surprise, the CEO had been waiting for Leah to ask for help. He never expected Leah to be perfect—but because Leah expected it of herself, she had avoided asking for the help she needed. If she had stayed in black-or-white thinking, Leah probably would have thought herself into an ulcer and out of a job. Instead, by trying on a shade of gray called "Good Enough (and Wanting It to Get Better)" Leah gave herself the chance to grow into her job and enter into a new, healthier relationship with herself.

Julia Child never believed that exceptional cooking required perfection. She knew (and had ample anecdotal evidence—captured on film, no less) that she could drop a latke and be a wonderful cook who delighted viewers and eaters alike. What's *Shift your black-or-white thinking to* your latke moment? Leah's was admitting that she was in over her head. What have you let fall *shades of charcoal,* and fail—and still come back to cook another *slate, or smoke* day? And who in your life can you let off the hook by shifting your black-or-white thinking to shades of charcoal, slate, or smoke? Julia herself once said, "Everything in moderation—including moderation."

For Michael and me, the question remained: Could you be a stellar parent while still giving your child an imperfect remedy? Well, last year, I was reading a popular parenting magazine when I came upon a column advising that, in a pinch, you could substitute saline eye drops for saline nose drops. I initially thought it was good enough that just I knew it. But then I realized that, in order to be a great wife, I needed to let Michael know—and put an end to a full decade of teasing from me. Not a perfect wife. But certainly good enough—and hopefully, getting better every day.

ACTION PLANNER

In the words of the French Enlightenment writer Voltaire, "The perfect is the enemy of the good." In the words of Coach Deb, here are some questions to think about as you consider whether good enough is good enough for your next undertaking:

What do you want?

_____

_____

_____

_____

What's at stake here?

_____

_____

_____

_____

What would "perfect" look like?

_____

_____

_____

_____

_____

What would "good enough" look like?

_____

_____

_____

_____

What "if-then" scenarios frighten you?

_____

_____

_____

What evidence do you have—no matter how small—that your "if-then" could turn out some other way than the worst-case scenario you have imagined? What similar setback have you survived—and can learn from here?

_____

_____

_____

_____

_____

_____

_____

_____

How might coming to terms with being "good enough" rather than "perfect" make your life easier?

_____

_____

_____

_____

_____

Who else has a say or stake in the standards you are setting for yourself?

_____

_____

_____

_____

_____

_____

What standards can you lower?

_____

_____

_____

_____

_____

What will it take to get started to be good enough? When will you get started?

_____

_____

_____

_____

_____

How will you know when you're at "good enough"?

_____

_____

_____

_____

_____

15

Climbing Life's Mount Sinai

ELEANOR ROOSEVELT famously remarked, "No one can make you feel inferior without your consent." Nobody, that is, except for my nine-year-old daughter, Sophie, who sat next to me at the breakfast table gleefully mastering a week's worth of *New York Times* math puzzles, while I thumbed through the Arts and Leisure section, looking for the latest Judd Apatow movie review.

"Mom," Sophie interrupted my reading. "Can you help me with this one?"

That was a good question. Could I help her? I didn't know if I would be able to help my child with a math puzzle geared for grown-ups. I also wasn't sure if I wanted to find out.

"I don't know if I can," I admitted, wondering if my brief junior high school stint as a mathlete would serve me twenty-five years later.

"Mom," Sophie pressed once again. *"Would* you help me with this one?"

Would I help? Now, that was an entirely different question. While I had my doubts that I could help, I certainly was willing to give it a try. The good news was that I was able to give her a small amount of direction to get her unstuck, and with that little bit of information, she aced yet another puzzle. The better news is that Sophie knew that I was willing to offer my assistance whether or not my assistance would prove fruitful. The best news? For me, it was that I actually could do something that I had written off as a "couldn't."

Over the years, I have learned to distinguish for myself, my family, and my clients the critical difference between two key behavioral barriers: "can't" and "won't." Both of these roadblocks can lead to frustration among colleagues, a chasm between expectations and outcomes, and a to-do list that never gets done. When something isn't getting accomplished, isn't getting accomplished well, or isn't getting accomplished quickly enough, it's time to channel your inner Sherlock Holmes and start investigating.

Columbia Business School professor Sheena Iyengar, author of *The Art of Choosing,* recounts her frustrating experience in Japan trying to order a cup of green tea. When her tea arrived, she politely asked the waiter for some sugar. He promptly rejected the request. Was he unable to? Was he unwilling? His response provided the first clue: "We don't put sugar in green tea." Aha—it was a "won't." Understanding that a Japanese cultural norm was at issue, Iyengar respectfully remarked that in her native India, green tea is often enjoyed sweet. Once again, the waiter refused to bring sugar. When Iyengar persisted, the waiter brought the manager to the table, who declared, "We don't have sugar." The "won't" had suspiciously morphed into a "can't." Now it seemed that it was less an issue of willingness and more an issue of inability due to a lack of needed resources. Iyengar, unable to procure a cup of green tea to her liking, threw up her hands and ordered a cup of coffee. When the coffee arrived, what was sitting on the saucer? You guessed it—two packets of sugar.

Channel your inner Sherlock Holmes and start investigating why you're stuck

As a social scientist, Iyengar knew that the barriers she faced in getting her wants and needs met were complex. When we find ourselves getting stuck—whether it's on a math puzzle or a life makeover—we need to become our own social scientists and ask ourselves:

- Am I facing a "can't"?

or

- Am I facing a "won't"?

"Can't"

"Can't do" represents a lack of ability, expertise, experience, or resources. I often work with Jewish private schools whose board members are excited to have a new mission and vision for their schools, and choose to bring me in to facilitate the process. Sometimes, the board members simply do not have the facilitation skills needed to get the school from where it is to where they want it to be, and the stakes are too high for them to risk the process or the outcome. Other times, I am invited to lead this process because, while certain board members could do it—they have the knowledge, skills, and experience needed—they won't do it because their strong opinions could cloud the facilitation process. I use inquiry, active listening, visioning, goal setting, and creating accountabilities so that, by the end of the process, the school has a new mission and vision. But even more importantly, many of the board members have learned some critical skills along the way so that their "can't" becomes a "can" for future projects of a similar nature.

"Can't" might morph into "can" over time. It could result from the development of critical skills and experiences needed to accomplish the task. It could also result from the simple passage of time. Chances are, if you work in an organization, you've had a terrific idea and the knowledge, skill, and ability to execute it, but you didn't have the resources (time, money) or permission (support from the team or the boss), so it was a "can't." Your task, then, became thinking strategically about how you might obtain the resources and agreement you needed to turn the "can't" into a "can." Or your task could have been to postpone it until the variables changed. Or to forget it altogether. Or to take the idea out on your own.

Whatever your goal or dilemma, whether you can or can't, those choices are up to you: to your level of investment, to your energy level, and to your appetite for risk for this particular roadblock.

Confronting "can'ts" is not just a modern-day challenge. We've seen this tension since biblical times. When God asked Moses to lead the Jewish people and transmit God's messages to them, Moses claimed a "can't." He described himself as a poor orator, afflicted with a speech impediment, and pulled in brother Aaron to become his mouthpiece. I'm a big Moses fan (I have all his books), but I think his "can't" was really a "won't." While "can't" is about ability, "won't" is about lack of motivation and confidence. He didn't want to speak because he didn't feel confident about his speaking—and perhaps even lacked the motivation to take on such a public role or to try to enhance his skills. But while Moses may not have been the most gifted speaker, he could speak if pressed to do so, as is evident many times in the Torah.

Now, I can't say that I blame Moses. He had a tricky childhood, he was shouldering the responsibility of an entire people, and he had a boss who managed by death threats. He may not have wanted to risk a poor performance when utter humiliation in front of an entire nation was the *least* brutal outcome. But where the costs for facing our "can'ts" are likely lower, it's worth considering whether we're really, truly unable to do something or entertaining the slight possibility that we're making Mount Sinais out of molehills.

"Won't"

Often, when it comes to unwillingness, we are our own worst enemy. There's no boss to blame or lack of opportunity at which we can throw up our hands and say, "Oh, well!" It's a battle between you and yourself—and chances are, you are both equally stubborn. When it comes to motivation, you may crave a particular outcome— but until you persuade yourself to do something, it's not going to get done. (And yes, sometimes the case can be as simple as, "I just don't want this hanging over me anymore.") Knowing your core values (such as achievement, recognition, contribution, or even fun), and aligning the process and outcome of your unpalatable activity with one of those, can be the spoonful of sugar that helps the medicine go down.

Moses had a tricky childhood—and a boss who managed by death threats

For me, my core value of competition helps motivate me to get my writing done, which is a painstaking, lonely task. I make a deadline and then work to beat that deadline. Being in a race—even when I am only besting my own expectations—drives me to complete the work sooner rather than later. Exercise is another tooth-pulling task for me, and I rely on my core value of fun, which shows up in the mindless form of *People, Us Weekly,* and other magazines, to get me moving. I only permit myself to indulge in brain candy when I am on the tread-mill or the elliptical machine. If I want to know whether Brad and Angelina have had another child, I have to hop on a piece of workout equipment to find out. As comedian Milton Berle once remarked, "Motivation is when your dreams put on work clothes!"

We all know that life requires us to do the things we don't want to do—especially when there are so many things that are easier and more fun. Why write when I could watch TV? Why work out when I could surf the web?

In their book, *Willpower,* authors Roy F. Baumeister and John Tierney recognize that our motivation is tested far more often than we give ourselves credit for. In fact, their research shows that most of us spend about a quarter of our waking hours resisting the temp-tation to do something else—anything else that's more desirable.

The most commonly resisted urge was eating (and even writing that makes me crave a cookie), followed by the impulse to sleep, closely trailed by the drive to take a break from work. When you think about this—that we spend close to four hours a day wishing we were doing something else—it makes sense that getting ourselves revved up to accomplish something can be a challenge.

According to Baumeister and Tierney, our frequent unwillingness to do what we don't want to do (or our inability to resist doing what we would rather do instead) comes at a cost. Think about this: Does indulging your "don't want tos" lead you to spend more money than you should? Waste time at work? Put off important personal goals? Keep you sedentary? Add to your stress level? Impact your interpersonal relationships? If you said yes to any of these, then your lack of will is getting in your way.

Baumeister and Tierney found that we need motivation to help us control four areas of life:

1. The thoughts that tell us that we can't do something or that we don't need to do something, and those thoughts that run on an endless loop keeping us from doing what we need to do.

2. The emotions that make us feel angry, stressed, reluctant or ashamed—without resorting to eating, drinking, shopping, gambling or otherwise "medicating" our emotions away.

3. Our impulses—our ability to resist those temptations listed above, as well as many others that we face all day long, such as checking our e-mail.

4. Our performance, such as managing our time, energy, efficiency, and efficacy, and sticking to it when our motivation is flagging.

Studies show that setting one specific improvement goal at a time is more likely to yield positive results than tackling several at once. Think about someone you know who tried to quit smoking and lose weight at the same time. They were probably on an emotional roller coaster—the emotional equivalent of Disney World's Space Mountain. On this roller coaster in the dark, you never know when the next turn or the next drop is, when you'll climb up, speed up, slow down, or come to a screeching halt. Tackling more than one major challenge that requires you to manage your motivation is more than most of us can achieve successfully.

My core value of competition helps motivate me to get my writing done

When it comes to managing our "won'ts," we also have to practice the skill of will. We need to practice controlling one thing that we aren't used to controlling and do it every day. Whether it's saying no to a second cup of coffee in the morning, turning off the TV at 10:00 p.m. to get some much-needed rest, or doing anything that is a little bit hard and (at least) a little bit meaningful, we can train our motivation muscles to be stronger and fitter so that they're less sore when we use them in the future and ready for whenever we do need them.

We also need to be strategically picky. While some people seem to have an unlimited reserve of motivation (and we either totally admire or completely loathe those people), most of us have our limits. Decide what you really, truly need to get motivated about—because it's important for you or important for someone who impacts your life—and apply your motivation there. Study a subject in which you're interested, start exercising, or stop swearing around your children. Eventually you may get to most of your goals, but don't aim to meet them all today. Set thoughtful, reasonable priorities, and use your motivation to achieve those.

Is there more to managing our "can'ts" and our "won'ts"? Of course there is. Using the worksheet below is a good start to discovering what that is.

ACTION PLANNER

Step 1: Name Your Goals and Your Barriers:

Goals	Impact	Can't	Won't
In my personal life, I'd like to achieve:	*If I accomplished this, I would have more/feel more:*	*I can't because:*	*I don't want to because:*
In my professional life, I'd like to achieve:	*If I accomplished this, I would have more/feel more:*	*I can't because:*	*I don't want to because:*
In my professional/ volunteer organization, I'd like to achieve:	*If I accomplished this, I would have more/feel more:*	*I can't because:*	*I don't want to because:*
In my family/ significant relationship, I'd like to achieve:	*If I accomplished this, I would have more/feel more:*	*I can't because:*	*I don't want to because:*

Step 2: Review the "Can't" Barriers:

Goals	My "can't"	What barrier is this?	What can I do about this? What can I do anyway?
In my personal life, I'd like to achieve:	I can't because:	☐ Education/ Training Skill ☐ Credential ☐ Opportunity ☐ Permission ☐ Resource ☐ Other _____	
In my professional life, I'd like to achieve:	I can't because:	☐ Education/ Training Skill ☐ Credential ☐ Opportunity ☐ Permission ☐ Resource ☐ Other _____	
In my professional/ volunteer organization, I'd like to achieve:	I can't because:	☐ Education/ Training Skill ☐ Credential ☐ Opportunity ☐ Permission ☐ Resource ☐ Other _____	
In my family/ significant relationship, I'd like to achieve:	I can't because:	☐ Education/ Training Skill ☐ Credential ☐ Opportunity ☐ Permission ☐ Resource ☐ Other _____	

Step 3: Review the "Won't" Obstacles:

Goals	My "won't"	What do I care about that I can use to motivate me:	What kind of self-control/willpower will I need for this?
In my personal life, I'd like to achieve:	*I am reluctant to because:*	*The process of doing it?* _____ *The outcome of getting it done?* _____	
In my professional life, I'd like to achieve:	*I am reluctant to because:*	*The process of doing it?* _____ *The outcome of getting it done?* _____	
In my professional/ volunteer organization, I'd like to achieve:	*I am reluctant to because:*	*The process of doing it?* _____ *The outcome of getting it done?* _____	
In my family/ significant relationship, I'd like to achieve:	*I am reluctant to because:*	*The process of doing it?* _____ *The outcome of getting it done?* _____	

Step 4: Review, Reject, and Select

Take a few minutes to look at your "Can't" and "Won't" lists. Make a note of which items seem most pressing. Maybe there's an opportunity that you know you need to seize now but you don't have the will to get started. Perhaps there's a project that you want to tackle but are missing some key skills to getting it done. Explain why you picked what you did and create a plan to get there.

I would like to take on this goal:

_____

The positive impact could be:

_____

The "can't" barriers I need to manage include:

_____

Here's what I will do to manage them:

_____

The "won't" obstacles I need to manage include:

_____

Here's what I will do to manage them:

_____

Keep in mind that you have another choice to make. Sometimes overcoming the "can't" or the "won't" may have emotional, financial, or interpersonal costs that are so high that the roadblock isn't worth knocking down or jumping over. In that case, your "can't" becomes a well-justified "won't." For example, your worksheet might reveal that you can't leave your job just now because you can't afford to. Well, you *could* leave, but you won't right now because it would put you and your family at risk. So, you honor the "can't" while you plan for the future. Give yourself permission to honor the roadblocks of skill or will that are too dangerous right now to overcome.

Keep in mind that if you're honoring a roadblock, you may need some support to help you deal with your current state on a daily basis.

What goal are you not going to tackle right now?	What's the potential for harm in tackling it?	What can you do in the meantime?	When would you like to revisit it?

Whatever you choose, you are in charge. And if you find that you don't or won't love the path you've picked, then find one that you can!

16

Your Laptop or Your Life!

What you are about to read may contain graphic descriptions and disturbing recommendations. Reader discretion is advised.

Within ninety seconds of entering my room at the Baltimore Hilton, where I was speaking at a conference, I realized that something was wrong: my laptop was missing.

I had clipped my laptop bag to my suitcase and checked my bag with the bellman when I arrived early that morning. But when I finally brought my suitcase to my room, I saw that it was no longer attached. Despite wanting to kick off my shoes and rest for a bit between sessions, I knew that I was now racing the clock. My cheery cherry laptop contained my presentation for the conference, of course, as well as every other document and contact I needed in order to function.

This was not a test of my emergency broadcast system. This was the real deal.

I raced down to the bag-check room as quickly as my platform pumps could carry me. Once there, heart pounding, I smiled and told the attendant exactly what had happened: my laptop had been attached to my suitcase, and now it was gone. Within three minutes, the team working the overloaded bag-check room had found my laptop and handed it over to me. I am not exaggerating when I say that I felt my life force return to my soul.

While walking back to the elevator bank, with my laptop case clutched in my sweaty palm, I realized that losing my computer would have stunk—big time—but it wasn't the most important thing in the world.

Here's the rub: I often act like it is.

Whether it's my laptop or my iPhone, too often I pay more attention to my technology than to my family. I tend to treat my toys with more tenderness than my kids. And I know that, after the kids are asleep, my e-mail gets more intimate eye contact from me than my husband does.

I know that I'm not alone. I also know that I am a carrier of this obsessive behavior, passing it down to the next generation—a generation that the Henry J. Kaiser Family Foundation has labeled "Generation M," for this group's ability to multitask and engage with media. In its 2005 report, "Generation M: Media in the Lives of 8-18 Year-Olds," the foundation described how children are surrounded and bombarded by technology everywhere they turn:

> New homes come complete with special nooks for oversized TV screens and home entertainment centers, while new cars come with personal TV screens in the back of each seat. The amount of media a person used to consume in a month can be down-loaded in minutes and carried in a device the size of a lipstick tube. Today we get movies on cell phones, TVs in cars, and radio through the Internet. Media technologies themselves are morphing and merging, forming an ever-expanding presence throughout our daily environment. Cell phones alone have grown to include video game platforms, e-mail devices, digital cameras and Internet connections.

Here's the bottom line: Many of our kids are spending over fifty hours a week—more than seven hours a day—plugged in. As the report points out, that's the equivalent of a full-time job plus overtime. But wait! There's more! The study shows that about 25 percent of that time is spent multitasking on more than one form of technology. "So what?" you may declare. "They are turning into gifted multitaskers!"

Not so fast, says David E. Meyer, director of the Brain, Cognition, and Action Laboratory at the University of Michigan. He found that when people try to perform two or more related tasks—either at the same time or alternating rapidly between them—both completion time and mistakes increase compared to unitask- *Too often I pay* ing. "The toll in terms of slowdown is extremely *more attention to* large—amazingly so," he remarks. Meyer found *my technology* that Generation M, despite a reputation for being *than to my family* master multitaskers, performs as poorly as the rest of us do when we try to engage in two cognitive activities at once. "If a teenager is trying to have a conversation on an e-mail chat line while doing algebra, she'll suffer a decrease in efficiency, compared to if she just thought about algebra until she was done. People may think otherwise, but it's a myth." Myth: That's an important new M for this generation, as well as for our own.

Technology overstimulates us at any age. While a cup of coffee may boost our productivity, too much of any stimulant starts to negatively impact our performance. Our brains need to rest and recover to review what we've learned and to plan ahead. But when any of us—no matter how old we are—are constantly stimulated by games, movies, TV, e-mail, texting, and more, our brains are too charged up to recharge. Eventually, as Meyer says, "People lose the skill and the will to maintain concentration, and they get mental antsyness." Simply put: we can no longer focus.

But I was still able to focus—and I was focused on the suspicion that I was, at best, repeatedly and flagrantly violating the First Commandment, *"You shall have no other gods before Me."* My e-toys were my gods, and I was bowing down before them on a daily—sometimes hourly—basis.

At worst, I was struggling with a "soft addiction." In her book, The Soft Addiction Solution, Judith Wright defines these as "those seemingly harmless habits like over-shopping, overeating, watching

I was struggling with a "soft addiction" too much TV, endlessly surfing the internet, procrastinating—that actually keep us from the life we want. They cost us money, rob us of time, numb us from our feelings, mute our consciousness, and drain our energy."

Constantly engaging in online activities gives me a high. But like all highs, there's a crash that follows, and only the next "refresh" of my browser will give me that good feeling all over again. I don't want to miss a thing online—a Facebook post, a Tweet, an e-mail—and this drive has cost me time and trust with the people who really need me off-line: my family.

My daughter, Sophie, has called me on this more than once: "You love your iPhone more than you love me." While we both know that this couldn't possibly be true, we also both see where my screen time is, at times, self-indulgent, self-aggrandizing, and just plain selfish.

Leave it to Sophie to bottom-line the right prescription: "You need some Techno-Bismol!"

She was right—I needed to unplug more often, so that I could plug into what and who really matters. Even Timothy Ferriss, bestselling author of *The 4-Hour Workweek,* believes that it's both possible and optimal to disconnect. "The single greatest enemy of creativity is overload," he says. "I believe creativity requires a relaxed acuity, which is rendered impossible by checking email every half hour."

So, what would I be willing to do that would also make a noticeable difference?

There are some extreme remedies for sure, and journalist Susan Maushart tried one of them, which she chronicled in her book, *The Winter of our Disconnect.* The subtitle says it all: "How Three Totally Wired Teenagers (and a Mother Who Slept with Her iPhone) Pulled the Plug on Their Technology and Lived to Tell the Tale." (The subtitle alone was a test of my ability to focus). She recounts: "When I first announced my intention to pull the plug on our family's entire armory of electronic weaponry—from the ittiest bittiest iPod Shuffle to my son's seriously souped-up gaming PC (the computing equivalent of a Dodge Ram)—my three kids didn't blink an eye. Looking back, I can understand why. They didn't hear me."

That's right. Her kids were so busy uploading pictures, commenting on Facebook, and watching YouTube that they didn't even hear the fate about to befall them for the next six months!

I wasn't about to go to those extremes, but here's what I did do: I committed to stop using my computer or checking e-mail on my iPhone from the time my kids got home from school until they went to bed at night.

Now before you argue "I can't do that because…," let me finish.

- It works for me because my friends and family can call me if they need me, and I can screen my calls so I know which ones to take.

- It works for me because I'm not a doctor, I don't work on Wall Street, and I don't have clients who, if they can't reach me for several hours, are risking their lives or livelihoods.

- It works for me because my husband and I are very mean and controlling (the tween-set's interpretation) and make our exhausted twins go to bed by 8:30 p.m.

Most importantly, it works for me because I told the kids that I was committed to doing this, and I asked them to hold me to my word. Have you ever invited your kids to catch you doing the wrong thing? Their attention, motivation, and commitment go through the roof. It's like watching them search for the *afikoman*—the hidden matzah—on Red Bull.

I custom designed this plan for me and my family. I'm not saying that you have a problem. I am just wondering aloud if other people in your life want more eye contact, ear contact, and human contact. And if so, what's your dose of "Techno-Bismol" going to look like? You won't find it on Google. You'll find it in your gut.

ACTION PLANNER

1. How would you rate your use of technology?

☐ Healthy—It doesn't interfere with my personal relationships, I'm not having trouble focusing on one thing at a time, and I'm not overly dependent on any of my devices.

☐ Mixed—Sometimes I manage my habits healthfully, and sometimes I don't.

☐ Addicted—When I'm not connected, I'm constantly thinking about my next opportunity for a "hit."

2. How is your current use of technology serving you? What does it make possible, better, or easier for you?

_____

_____

_____

3. What does your current use of technology allow you to avoid?

_____

_____

_____

Let's imagine. What would happen if you...	The worst thing that could happen	The best thing that could happen	Will I try it? (Yes/No)
...experimented with short periods of inaccessibility?			
... left your mobile device at home one day a week?			
...left your mobile device at work one night a week?			
...didn't check e-mail after work?			
...created and enforced your own rules about technology use?			
...created and enforced rules about your kids' technology use?			
...told your staff that you expected them to "unplug" at home—even one night a week?			
...got a buddy to do this with you?			

17

Take a Sabbath for Your Soul

I AM WRITING THIS while lying facedown on a table at the elegant Green Massage Spa in Shanghai's World Financial Center. There is a fuchsia flower floating in a black lacquered bowl on the floor as a retreat for my eyes and a petite lady with deceptively aggressive elbows digging into the kinks in my upper back. Since I knew better than to try to bring my laptop in for the signature Thai-style massage, I am writing this in my head. And as my dainty, deft masseuse finds all the right knots in all the usual spots—That's it!—she admonishes me: "Very bad!"

We haven't known each other long enough for her to comment on my driving or my dancing. And since this is my third massage in as many weeks, I have come to expect those two words being tsk-tsk'd at me by someone whose job it is to help me release my tension. I know exactly what those two words mean: You are not relaxed.

This is not news—not to me, or to anyone who knows me. I don't really have an "off" button, or if I do, where it lies is a mystery wrapped inside an enigma enveloped in puff pastry smothered in the secret sauce my mother uses for her brisket.

I understand perfectly well that relaxation is an essential element to staying healthy in body, mind, and soul. Relaxation gives us the time and space we need to reconnect with ourselves, with our friends and families, with our values and priorities, and, if we choose, with God. He surely knew what He was doing when he commanded—not suggested, hinted, or implied—that we were to rest on the Sabbath day. As Naomi Levy writes in *To Begin Again:* "Even the most harried workdays become tolerable when you know a day of holy peace is shortly arriving. The days succeeding the day of rest become days of light too. They shimmer with the afterglow of a revived spirit."

Yet I struggle, really struggle, in my quest to slow down.

When Michael and I got married, he knew that he would be giving up his right to date other people, to ever choose our Saturday night movie, or to stretch out beyond his wafer-thin section of the bed.

My husband was sacrificing one of his inalienable rights— the right to nap

What he didn't expect was that he would be sacrificing one of his (assumed) inalienable rights—the right to nap. Michael has asked me repeatedly over the past thirteen years, "How come I can't nap just because *you* don't believe in napping?" It's a valid question, worthy of consideration and response, and I can always find something to do (Let's make our Shabbat dinner invitation list for the year!) to avoid answering it.

Over the years, I have introduced many of my work colleagues and clients to Michael. It's a fair assumption that most people who know me from leading workshops or from speaking engagements notice the energy, enthusiasm, and passion I bring to my work. I love what I do with every ounce of my being, and it shows. But I have noticed that when these same people meet Michael, they ask him some variation of, "What's she like at home?" I believe this question combines both admiration and abject pity for my husband. They want to know if I shut off, shut down, or shut up. Michael, ever the loyalist, just smiles. We both know the answer. I'm starting to think this guy might deserve a nap.

Now, in my defense, I come by this honestly. My mother, Nancy, at age sixty-something, makes me seem positively slothlike. She is a whirling dervish of activity. She is usually planning a party, hosting a party, cleaning up from a party, or attending a party. As a publisher of high-end brochures for wedding and special event venues, she is at her desk by sunup, speaking and meeting with clients all day, running errands in between, calling or seeing her thirteen grandchildren, and working again until midnight. When I tell people that my mother lives in Florida, they ask, "Oh, is she retired?" "Never!" I exclaim. A few years after my stepfather, Ron, and my mother got married, he asked me, "Does she ever stop? Will I ever be allowed to rest?" I gave him the same sad smile that Michael gives my colleagues. We both know the answer.

In my mother's defense, she comes by this honestly. Her mother, my grandma Olga, was diagnosed with multiple sclerosis when my mom was a young child. By the time my mother was a teenager, her mother was paralyzed and bedridden. My mother spent most of her years with a mother who couldn't actively participate in life the way that either of them would have wanted. So my mom chose to live the most energetic and dynamic life she could, to make up for what she didn't have.

While she had no role model and I had the ultimate role model for living a nonstop life, I think we could both benefit from learning how to power down. (I'll let Ron broach that with her—I don't want to lose my invitation to Florida for President's Week.)

According to Gerald Rosen in *The Relaxation Book* (perfect for those of us who need help even picturing what powering down might look like), relaxation is important because it allows us to manage our complex environments. While our day-to-day stresses and strains may vary, most of us are faced with meeting multiple demands on a regular basis. Reducing our own stress through respite enables us to meet our responsibilities more efficiently and effectively. Rosen cites a variety of relaxation techniques, including meditation, yoga, and, lucky for me, massage.

Regardless of what kind of relaxation any of us chooses (or struggles to commit to), Rosen recommends that in order for the activity to really renew and recharge us, it needs to meet four criteria:

1. **A quiet environment.** This could be a room in your home, a calm spot at the office, your car, or a place of worship. You should feel tranquil and free from sound and sight distractions.

2. **A comfortable position.** Sit up or recline in a way that has you avoiding any discomfort or muscle tension. If lying down fosters your relaxation, then by all means do so—just know that you might fall asleep (like some people to whom I am married).

3. **A mental device.** This can be a phrase that you repeat to yourself, a word, or even a sound. It could also include slow breathing, slow movement (like in tai chi), or even a soft, fixed gaze on an object. It could also be an open-ended question that allows you to focus inwardly. An example would be chanting, "Shalom. Shalom. Shalom." Or asking, "What gives me peace?"

4. **A nonjudgmental attitude that allows us to ignore distractions and focus on our mental device.** This is key to making the other steps work. It is highly likely that distractions will occur—whether they are external stimuli, like the phone ringing, or diverting thoughts, like wondering when the phone is going to ring. In order for relaxation to occur, we must neither judge the distraction nor give it deep consideration. Our mental state should permit us to notice the distraction (pretending not to takes hard work, which is counteractive to relaxation) and then let it go so that we can refocus and recapture our mental device.

For my husband, a nap meets these four criteria beautifully. For me, a nap might meet criteria one and two, but my phrase would be, "There's too much to do and not enough time!" repeated over...and over...and over again. This is not the kind of mantra that researchers recommend. With criterion three feeling impossible to achieve, working toward number four seems like a waste of time. So I need a different form of relaxation. Clearly, one man's nap is another one's breeding ground for anxiety!

Fortunately, Rosen lets me off the hook a bit. He writes that learning to relax is an ability, not an instant fix. It's a learned set of skills that, like anything else, benefits from practice.

One neuroscience study from the Massachusetts Institute of Technology made the case for taking breaks from the "rat race" even stronger. Scientists David Foster and Matthew Wilson "eavesdropped" on the brain processes of rats as they explored their environments. They discovered that the rats use their resting time to replay their exploration experiences—increasing their recall and intensi- *Relaxation allows us to manage our complex environments* fying their learning. When the rats took their siestas, their brain cells replayed the exact sequence of electrical firing over and over, only in reverse and speeded up. They were experiencing an "instant replay" of sorts that could be used to lock in critical learning. And what could this mean for us? It could mean that relaxation holds an additional benefit for us: it's an opportunity for our human brains to replay and learn from recent experiences.

I, on the other hand, still had plenty to learn about how to break through my drive for busyness and get to the other side. And yes, it took a trip to the other side of the world for me to really come face-to-face with my resistance to inactivity. For a month each year, I live in China, half a world away from my family and friends in New York, to teach an MBA course. I know that I have to keep busy every day to avoid feeling a constant low-grade ache from missing my family.

Without me around to interfere with my family's ability to "just chill," they did exactly that. French fries were eaten in mass quantities. Wii was played with abandon. Beds were left unmade (which I know thanks to Skype video). It's possible that napping may have occurred. I have no proof, of course. Just my suspicions.

And since I didn't have to distract myself with activity, I started to practice something else: relaxing. My cooking facilities were primitive at best, so I ate out for dinner every night, slowly savoring sweet and sour Mandarin fish, salty-egg pumpkin, dumplings with cloud ear mushrooms, and stir-fried spinach with peanuts and garlic, washed down with coconut milk.

I didn't have television, so I stayed up late reading wonderful books, listening to music on my iPod, and writing notes to my family and friends.

I also had more spa treatments in my month in China than I had had in my entire life. With body therapies starting at less than ten dollars an hour, I luxuriated in an eighty-minute foot massage that began with a rose-petal foot bath and a chilled cup of Macao-style cream pudding (for my mouth, not my feet) and ended in sheer bliss. I visited a hot springs resort, where I soaked in baths filled with milk and flowers, red wine, and lavender and eucalyptus. I experienced Chinese cupping and Chinese scraping treatments (while both left marks behind, they weren't painful), and had my first solid night of sleep directly after. I had head massages, shoulder massages, and, of course, today's Thai massage.

Now, I know that if I carried on this way at home, I would quickly become broke, mammoth, and single. However, like Rosen's four criteria for relaxation, I wanted to create my own curriculum for bringing serenity back home with me:

1. I want to be aware when I am using "doing" to avoid "feeling."

2. I want to honor my kids' desire to chill out, without judgment, guilt, or retribution.

3. I want to be more sensitive to my own need for and ability to relax.

And most importantly,

4. I want my husband, Michael, to take as many naps as he wants. Lord knows, the guy has earned them.

So while my masseuse may scorn me for my knotted neck and stiff shoulders, I know that just lying here on this table, staring down at the flower between her feet, is a big step for me. I am doing nothing. Just relaxing. Chilling out. And, of course, writing this chapter in my head.

Hey, it's a start.

ACTION PLANNER

How do you currently cope with life's stressors?

_____

_____

_____

What methods are most successful for you? What makes them successful?

_____

_____

_____

What benefits would having more relaxation in your life bring you?

_____

_____

_____

_____

_____

How important are those benefits to you? Why?

_____

_____

_____

_____

_____

_____

What are you willing to say "no" to in order to say "yes" to more relaxation?

_____

_____

_____

_____

_____

_____

What relaxation activities could you start incorporating that meet Gerald Rosen's four criteria:

Relaxation Activity	In what quiet environment could this activity take place? How could I make it quieter?	What position will be most comfortable for me?	What word, phrase, sound, object, breathing, or movement will I focus on as a mental device?	What distractions could I reasonably anticipate? What can I do to minimize them? How will I push them away if they arise?

18

How to Get a Move On Moving On

SOPHIE, AGE SEVEN, was devastated. Her twin brother, Jacob, had just announced the name of the six-year-old girl he was going to marry, and Sophie disapproved of his choice. It was not surprising that Jacob picked someone who was Sophie's polar opposite—and who drove her bananas—while Jacob found this young lady to be delightful and charming.

"What if she's not a good aunt to my kids?" Sophie demanded, projecting ahead (at least) twenty years.

"It's possible that she may mature in time," I suggested, trying to stay neutral.

"But what if she doesn't and then she teaches my kids bad behaviors?" Sophie pressed.

"It's possible, but what if Jacob doesn't end up marrying her?" I offered.

"But what if he does?"

"If he does, isn't it possible that twenty years from now, you might feel differently about her? You might not even remember that you didn't like her when you were kids!" I ventured.

Sophie considered this for a moment and then made her final decree. "I'll write myself a note!"

While Sophie might, over time, naturally move past the disappointment over her brother's potential, eventual *bashert,* she was already planning to be upset—for today and for at least two more decades.

I would have liked to chalk this up to her age, but I have personally known and professionally worked with enough adults to know that

Feelings can leave a lasting ink stain on our hearts, minds, and souls

people hang on to these "notes"—their reminders to stay angry, hurt, and disappointed—for decades. The writing on their notes may have faded years ago, but the feelings leave a lasting ink stain on their hearts, minds, and souls. Years and years pass, and many of us are still feeling sad and mad about the dream job we almost got, a fight with a family member where the distance between you remains, or the "one that got away" in our romantic life.

We all know that change and loss are inevitable. As author Judith Viorst wrote in *Necessary Losses:*

> When we think of loss, we think of the loss, through death, of people we love. But loss is a far more encompassing theme in our life. For we lose not only through death, but by leaving and being left, by changing and letting go and moving on. And our losses include not only our separations and departures from those we love, but our conscious and unconscious losses of romantic dreams, impossible expectations, illusions of freedom and power, illusions of safety—and the loss of our own younger self, the self that thought it would always be unwrinkled and invulnerable and immortal.

But alas, we hang on to many of life's painful situations, unmet needs, broken promises, crossed boundaries, and unfinished business simply because the illusion or hurt has become habit. For any of us who have ever tried to quit smoking, or to stop biting our nails, or to leave the Blackberry off during dinner, we know firsthand that breaking ingrained habits can be uncomfortable—even painful—so why bother?

Because when we choose to put our old frustrations, anxiety, and anger behind us, we release the time, energy, and productivity we need to make positive changes in our lives. Loss may be inevitable, but lamenting and lingering over many of these losses is optional.

Take Joseph—yes, *that* Joseph—the one with the colorful coat: He chose to move past the betrayal of his brothers, who faked his death and sold him off as a slave in response to their father's overwhelming favoritism. He lost his youth, his family, his freedom—and yet, he was able to move on. He *chose* to move on. He decided to end the old story in order to begin a new chapter—literally and figuratively—in his life, the lives of his brothers and father, and ultimately, in the lives of the Jewish people.

Sam, thirty-six, came to coaching with a vague goal of finding more fulfillment in life. He was missing something—that much he was aware of—but he didn't know exactly what that something was. As we spoke about which areas of his life needed more attention, Sam's romantic history came into full focus. When we discussed his dating past and present, Sam told me that he had had his heart broken by a romantic partner, Shana, four years earlier, and that he felt he should be over her, but he just wasn't. He replayed what went wrong in the relationship over and over in his mind during the day, dreamed about Shana many nights, and heard her voice on a never-ending loop in his head, telling him that he was undeserving of love.

Many of us have been rejected in the past, or felt unworthy, or have experienced the sting of unrequited love—and we have been able to put that behind us to move forward. Since Sam hadn't, I thought that he might be hanging on to a piece of history for some very good reasons.

"Sam," I asked, "You're pretty clear that thinking about Shana is getting in the way of your moving on in your personal life. I've found that many of us have attitudes and behaviors that seem not to serve us but somehow do anyway. Can you think about how keeping this old hurt alive may be helping you in some way?"

Sam thought about this for a few moments and then said, "I guess that thinking about Shana is protecting me from loving and losing someone again. As long as I'm engaging with Shana in my head, I'm not looking for someone else. And if I'm not looking, I'm not finding anyone. And if I'm not finding anyone, then there's nobody to lose."

"Sam, that sounds very honest—and totally exhausting. Is it?"

Sam breathed out audibly. "Yes. Yes it is exhausting. But there's more."

"I'm listening."

"I also feel like keeping Shana at the forefront of my mind keeps me connected to her—even though I know she doesn't want to be connected to me anymore. So I'm kind of doing something that she'd hate!" Sam scoffed, giving a little laugh. "That sounds crazy. Am I crazy?"

"Sam, I think you're sad, and hurt, and mad, and wanting both to keep this alive and have it be done with once and for all. Does that sound right?"

Sam said, "Yes, that sounds exactly right."

"Then that's not crazy. That's human!"

"Thank God!" Sam said and laughed. "But there's more."

"Go for it."

"I feel like the longer I stay mad at Shana, the more I feel like I am sending her the anger and agony she deserves. I feel like moving past it would be like letting her off the hook. But she's not on the hook!"

"You're right, Sam. She's not."

"I'm the only one on this hook. I'm keeping me there. I mean, I'm keeping me here."

"Where's 'here'?"

"In pain. Not moving forward. Not with anyone. I'm keeping me here."

"And where would you rather be?"

"I want to be married. I want to have kids!" Sam blurted out. "Oh, my goodness—I haven't admitted that to myself for years. And I certainly haven't said that out loud!"

"Wow, Sam. This is huge—and really important for moving on. How does it feel to say that—to yourself and to me?"

"Terrifying. Truthful."

"Yes, I can see why it would feel like both. So, Sam: You have this scary and real dream for yourself. You want a partner. A family. How ready do you feel to start extricating yourself from this 'hook' you're hanging on to?"

"I'm ready, but I can't just jump off the hook, or jump into the water, or whatever the metaphor is."

"So what *will* you do right now? What do you feel capable of doing that will get you closer to where you want to get to?"

Sam thought about it. "I want to write a letter to Shana and not send it. Sending it would be making a connection. And we're not connected. Or we're not anymore, other than in my head. I really can see that now."

"And what will you do with the note?"

Sam considered his options. "I don't want to keep it. Can I give it to you?"

Within a week, Sam had handwritten a letter and mailed it to me, and I keep it, still sealed, in my lower left-hand desk drawer, along with other people's reminders to themselves to release the grip they have on unrealized dreams and old hurts. As Rabbi Shira Milgrom shared in her Yom Kippur 5749 sermon, "Yes, it is life affirming to allow ourselves to feel—to feel pain. But it is anti-life to mourn without limit—to consume one's life in sadness."

How about you? Is there old news in your personal or professional life that is keeping you from starting new growth? And if so, how long do you want to hold on to it? Just remember that packing away your old notes may help you write a new chapter.

ACTION PLANNER

1. Think about a dream or a disappointment that still feels present and alive for you. Write down what happened below, as if you were telling someone else the story. Notice the primary emotions you are feeling as you write. Don't judge—just notice.

_____

_____

_____

_____

_____

_____

_____

2. In what ways is keeping this old business fresh and current feeding you? Does it protect you from having to take action? Does it make you feel justified in your actions or inactions?

_____

_____

_____

_____

_____

_____

_____

3. How would you feel if you moved on from this. Would it feel like you compromised your integrity? Your identity? Or might it feel like a huge weight has been lifted off your shoulders?

_____

_____

_____

_____

_____

4. How does keeping this old business fresh starve you? What are the costs to you? Sleep? Confidence? Your health? Fear?

_____

_____

_____

_____

_____

5. Nobody can make the decision about what to do next except for you. Do the benefits outweigh the costs? Or would you be better off eliminating or reducing the costs?

I would rather:

_____

_____

_____

6. If you have decided to let go of the old dream or disappointment, use the space below to draft a good-bye letter:

I am choosing to:

_____

_____

_____

The costs I am not willing to live with anymore include:

_____

_____

_____

I might want to let the following people know about my choice:

_____

_____

_____

It's okay if I still feel/do:

_____

_____

_____

If you have decided to "keep the old note," to stay frustrated, angry, or sad, that's a decision that you are entitled to make. You can revisit this choice anytime you feel that the costs outweigh the benefits.

19

Put Your Network to Work

GROWING UP IN MANHATTAN, I didn't need to learn how to drive. But after three years of living in Ann Arbor, Michigan, where buses and subways were no longer at my doorstep, it was time to learn. I passed my driver's test (because it didn't require me to parallel park), and bought a used red and white Plymouth Reliant K. My parents quickly bought me something they knew I would need to support my fledgling skill set—a membership in the American Automobile Association (AAA).

I was as new to driving as I was to car ownership, and, I must admit, I immediately put my AAA membership to good use. My AAA team helped me learn that it was a bad idea to park the car and leave the lights on so I could find it at night. My AAA team supported me in those pre-GPS days with a TripTik as I made the half-cross-country drive from Michigan to Washington, DC, for a summer job. And my AAA team found me great deals at hotels, movie theaters, and restaurants.

But AAA isn't just for drivers on the road. AAA is for anyone looking to steer his or her life and career in the right direction. How? Through the "Triple A" of networking:

- Approach (and Be Approachable)

- Ask a Great Question

- Add Value

Like AAA on the road, the AAA of networking can help you get the inside track, find direction in work and life, and yes, help you in case of emergency.

In his book, *The Guide for the Perplexed,* the great Jewish philosopher Moses Maimonides wrote that we are naturally social beings, and that, by virtue of our natures, we seek to form communities. He would know: as a doctor, rabbi, scholar, mathematician, astronomer, and writer, Maimonides must have been a member of multiple professional, academic, and social communities. Imagine how many business cards he had to carry!

> *We are naturally social beings and we seek to form communities*

Despite our natural drive to connect with others, we live in a world that's more competitive than ever. Whether you are looking to find or change a job, attract new customers, donors or volunteers, or bring new visibility and connections to your institution, you need to know that there are dozens, hundreds, thousands of people and businesses fighting for attention.

So, how do you stand out? How do you get your foot in the door? By the first A of networking: Approach (and Be Approachable). That refers to how you approach networking, as well as how you approach the people with whom you want to connect.

APPROACH

While you may not be looking for that perfect new job or contact today, you never know when a relationship you've built through networking will come in handy. How do I know? Because I have benefitted personally and professionally from planting the seeds that reap unbelievable rewards.

I had always thought that my job as a speaker, facilitator, and coach was allowing me about as much fun as you could have at work (and still have it be legal), until I got a request in the fall of 2009 that took fun to new heights: Would I be available to lead a two-day presentation skills course for the Beijing International MBA program at Peking University in China?

Yes, I think I can move a few things around to make that happen.

I also thought that I had the greatest friends in the world—until I started sharing the news about this assignment and kept hearing the refrain: "How did you get *that?*"

Of course, they quickly backpedaled: "I mean, I know you're really good and all, but still..."

Apparently, despite my twenty-plus years of training and experience, my friends' faith in my talents had a North American-shaped boundary.

Nevertheless, their faith in my networking talents exploded when I explained that I had gotten this incredible opportunity from Leslie, a training professional whom I had met at a networking event three years prior. On paper, Leslie and I would *What if we each became, over time, a trusted referral source to the other?* have been considered direct competition to each other. Leslie and I both do communication skills training, offering similar services to similar clients at similar price points. But Leslie and I had approached each other with a different mindset: What if we each became, over time, a trusted referral source to the other? Surely, each of us would have occasional scheduling conflicts. Wouldn't it be nice to be able to make a referral—while still maintaining the relationship with the client? Through our willingness, ability, and commitment to building a strategic and mutually beneficial relationship, Leslie and I have been rewarded personally and professionally dozens of times over.

That personal approach—and Leslie's and my approachability—is the start of real networking. Most of us recognize the importance of networking, but when it comes right down to it, we really don't know how to do it well. If you approach networking as showing up to as many events as possible, while subtly (or not so subtly) making the case for yourself or your business as you make the rounds, your approach isn't working. If you approach networking as basically random, casual conversation, your approach isn't working. If you approach networking as needing to be "on" all the time to be a good networker, your approach isn't working.

Those of us who go this route usually end up abandoning networking after attending too many parties and meetings with too few results—and then arrive at the conclusion that networking doesn't really work.

But it does. Regardless of where you live, the size of your community or city, or how long you've been in your job or industry, the key to effective networking is approaching it strategically.

One approach to networking that has worked for me—and my clients—is to think of it as a series of thoughtfully planned actions designed to lead to a particular goal. Begin by having a distinct purpose in mind, whether that objective is to advance your career, increase your client base, or raise the visibility of your organization. In strategic networking, the specific activities you choose will be in alignment with your overall goals. Like the other core competencies we need in order to advance ourselves, networking requires preparation, consideration, and intention. Effective networkers have a very clear picture of the desired outcome and implement a plan that boosts their chances of attaining that outcome.

ACTION PLANNER: APPROACH

Here are some reflection questions to help you think about what has worked for you in the past and how your past experience can lead to success in the future:

How do you personally define "networking"?

_____

_____

_____

When have you networked before? What were the outcomes?

_____

_____

_____

What particular strategies were most successful for you? Why?

_____

_____

_____

What particular strategies were not worth the time and effort? Why?

_____

_____

_____

How do you think your approach to networking has impacted your outcomes?

_____

_____

_____

What shifts in your approach could help you be more successful at it?

_____

_____

_____

What are your top three networking goals right now?

1. _____

2. _____

3. _____

Part of successful networking is knowing whom to approach, how, and why. The Talmud tells us, "Your friend has a friend and the friend of your friend has a friend." That's good news for us, especially these days. Traditionally, networking experts have cited that fewer than 15 percent of people find their jobs through print or online classifieds. When the economy is in a slump worldwide, that number is even lower. Most workers are "drafted" into organizations by friends, family, and colleagues. People choose with whom to do business based on referrals and recommendations. All of this lends credence to the age-old adage, "It's not what you know, it's who you know."

Consider this powerful statistic: Most people have at least 250 contacts. These contacts can be family, friends, clients, colleagues, former colleagues, classmates, fellow commuters, your exercise partners, vendors...the list is endless. If you know 250 people and each of those people knows 250 people, then the second level of your network contains over 62,000 people!

Does that sound overwhelming...or encouraging? If it sounds encouraging, then you're ready to dive right in. Either way, if you approach networking by breaking it down into bite-size chunks to make the process more manageable, then you are setting yourself up for success. And isn't that what networking is all about?

Organization is essential to successfully compile a contact list that is usable over time. Follow these five steps to create an extraordinary contact list:

1. Namestorm. Figuring out whom to approach is secondary to figuring out whom you already know. Begin by opening up a new document in your computer, using a pad of Post-it Notes, or a giant flip chart. You will need plenty of space to write down everyone you know—whether you know them intimately or by name only. At this point in the process, you want to separate generation from evaluation. In other words, focus on quantity here rather than quality. Consider this process to be "green-light" thinking—everything and anything goes! You will have time later to evaluate this list—but first things first.

Here are some categories to get you started namestorming:
- Friends
- Friends of friends
- Family members
- Friends of family members
- Parents of your children's friends
- Present colleagues

- Past colleagues
- Classmates
- Synagogue/house of worship members
- Recreational partners (sports, games, hobbies, etc.)
- Fellow commuters
- Personal service providers (hairdressers, spa technicians, etc.)
- Health care providers
- Financial service providers
- Vendors your company uses
- People you are connected to via Facebook, LinkedIn, or other social networking sites
- Members of professional organizations

What other categories would you add? Keep in mind that namestorming is an ongoing process—you can always add new contacts to this master list.

2. Prioritize your contact list. It's true you never know who can help you, but in order to maximize your time, you need to prioritize your list. You might begin by creating a chart that evaluates your contacts in two ways: first, by how well you know each person, and second, by how connected each person is to helping you meet your networking goals. (What networking goals? Go back to your worksheet if this is news to you!)

For example, your mother may be a close contact but may not be able to help you find an accounting position in an advertising firm in Seattle. A gentleman with whom you attend synagogue may not be a close contact, but you know that he is well connected in the Pacific Northwest. And if you're really lucky, you'll find that you have contacts who serve both needs!

Name	Close contact?	Connected to my goals?
Mother	Yes	No
Sam Birnbaum	No	Yes
Leslie Stern	Yes	Yes

Can you take a guess with which contact you would start?

Here's a blank table to get you started:

Name	Close contact?	Connected to my goals?	Notes

3. Organize your list. Your brain needs your help. Scraps of paper and Post-its scattered about will not help you—or your brain—get organized. Instead, set up a computer database that lists your contacts and all of their information. Include phone numbers, e-mail and snail mail addresses, fax numbers, and any other data you think is important. It doesn't hurt to include notes indicating where your contacts hang out, professional associations and societies to which they belong, and any special interests they have.

You can use programs such as Outlook or Excel to keep all your contact information together. In addition to setting up a database, you will need to create a tickler system or schedule to update your list on a regular basis. You might decide to update your database after every ten new contacts or business cards that you collect, or to do so on a weekly or biweekly basis.

4. Set up a schedule. Remember that staying in touch is a cornerstone of good networking. What doesn't get scheduled doesn't get done. Set up a schedule that helps you stay current, connected, and communicating—without becoming a pest. Plan for phone calls, e-mails, coffee, and other greetings to stay on people's proverbial radar screens. Too many people spend a ton of time compiling a hearty list of contacts, only to let it just sit there. Set some goals for yourself. For example, try contacting five people on your list per week or adding ten new people to your list per month.

Keep in mind that even before you approach people, you need to be strategic. You need to identify with whom you want to be speaking, why that person could be a good connection for you, how you might benefit one another, what you should be discussing, and when and where you could reconnect.

5. Use your database. Now that you have a list of people to approach, how do you go about approaching them? Is using Facebook a faux pas? Is LinkedIn for losers? Is face-to-face the favorite? It's often hard to know whether to go high-tech or high-touch. Of course, if you had all the time in the world, you could go to every networking event, breakfast meeting, cocktail party, or conference that came across your desk. If you had all the time in the world, you could stay in regular touch with important contacts through phone calls, lunch dates, or drinks (assuming that they had all the time in the world, too). If you had all the time in the world, you could cultivate relationships slowly, ensuring deep and lasting connections that would serve both of you. If you had all the time in the world, you could show me how to have it, too!

Assuming that we are bound by the limits of time and space, let's study our options. While there's no substitute for face-to-face interactions, there is a time, a place, and a purpose for going online for networking activities. Here are pros and cons to keep in mind for both:

Face-to-Face Networking

Pros:

1. If you have a great personality, face-to-face networking allows you to show it off. You are no longer the resume at the bottom of the stack; potential clients/ employers can put a name to a face.

2. It is easier to determine whether or not you think you'd like to work with an individual. The question, "Can I actually picture myself working with this person?" becomes easier to answer when you have spoken with someone in person rather than over the phone, through a series of e-mails, or on Facebook.

3. Networking can be fun, especially at a conference or cocktail party. You get to leave the house or office, dress up, and have a potentially stimulating conversation with a fellow like-minded adult. (This is particularly true for people who work from home, whether that work is paid or unpaid.)

4. You will make yourself more memorable. People are more likely to keep a "live" encounter in mind than a virtual one.

Cons:

1. Time Consuming. Networking events may last several hours and you must remember to factor in preparation and even travel time.

2. Can be costly. You must factor in:
   - Travel
   - Hotel
   - Rental car
   - Fee to attend conference
   - Taking off from work to attend the event
   - Paying for babysitter/daycare if you have children
   - Buying an appropriate outfit for the event

3. Mentally taxing. Face-to-face networking requires you to schmooze with potential clients/employers for long periods of time. You have to shake hands and engage in conversation that may or may not yield a positive outcome. You may also feel it necessary to reach out and e-mail each person with whom you spoke when you return home. It can be very draining to contact each person from whom you received a business card.

4. First impressions can be misleading. Many people become nervous or shy when put in situations where they must "sell" themselves. Potential employers may not get to see the "real you."

Online/Social Networking

Pros:

1. Because you are not restricted to a particular geographic region, you can reach people in different states, countries, or continents.

2. You can network 24-7. My colleagues in China are having breakfast while I am having dinner, but that doesn't stop us from reaching out to one another. If you are a morning person and wish to get some networking done in the early morning hours, you can send e-mails or comment on blogs at 6:00 a.m. without having to plan a meeting. If you prefer to work late at night, you can use social networking sites at midnight.

3. Makes it more likely that potential employers or clients will meet with you in person, as they feel like they already know you to some degree. This is a good reminder that your online persona requires as much care and attention as your off-line one does.

4. You can strengthen your connections by posting a comment on someone's Facebook wall or following her on Twitter. Contributing your ideas shows your dedication, involvement, and commitment to your line of work.

Cons:

1. It can be misleading. Someone who looks great on paper and has all of the right credentials may look great to work with. However, without that face-to-face interaction, it is often hard to tell.

2. It may reinforce stereotypes. Knowing only a select few details about a person (such as age, gender, race, highest level of education) may lead to incorrect conclusions. By limiting communication to social networking sites, you lose the opportunity to prove that you do not fit a stereotype.

Considering what you now know about the pros and cons of face-to-face and online/social networking, list five situations in which you would choose to go "high-touch" and five situations in which you would rather go "high-tech":

I will network in person when:

1. _____

2. _____

3. _____

4. _____

5. _____

I will network online when:

1. _____

2. _____

3. _____

4. _____

5. _____

Whether you network in person, online, or both, you want to make yourself approachable, accessible, and inviting. In other words, you want to be a "people person." Keep this in mind: many of us think a "people person" is someone who is energetic and lively, and who can make small talk with ease and enjoys doing it. If this isn't you, don't worry. Everyone is a "people person"—just to different kinds of people. You might find yourself naturally drawn to, or drawing in, people who are analytical, reserved, or methodical. You might be just the right match for someone who is zany, fast-paced, or outgoing.

As long as you are genuine, as well as genuinely interested in learning more about the people around you, you can become an effective networker no matter what your natural style is.

And no matter whether you're quick or slow, upbeat or reserved, the quickest way to make yourself approachable is with a warm smile and great eye contact. Research shows that smiling is contagious (there's finally something we don't want Purell to kill). *Avot D'Rabbi Natan* (a companion volume in the Talmud to *Pirkei Avot*) says, "One who welcomes his friend with a smile gives him the finest gift in the world." And what if she isn't a friend yet? What an easy way to make one!

Great eye contact requires a careful balancing act between too long and too short. Eye contact that is too long is awkward: a stare-down can signify that you're ready for a brawl in the parking lot or that you're locking eyes in preparation for locking lips. Neither is appropriate for networking, and eye contact that borders on gawking or glaring labels you as a loose cannon—probably not what you're going for to make great business or community connections.

Eye contact that is too short is just as bad. How many times have you been speaking with someone and you notice his eyes looking past you, scanning the room for someone else—perhaps someone better —to come along? Or maybe she's stealing a glance at her iPhone. (And how many times have you been the offender?) No matter what the distraction, furtive glances make you look shifty, absentminded, or untrustworthy—none of which is the kind of impression you want to make.

Even if you think there's someone in the room who may be a better match for your needs and interests, you do yourself and others a disservice by not giving everyone the chance to approach—or be approached. In *Pirkei Avot,* Rabbi Meir said: "Look not at the container but at what it contains; there may be a new flask full of old wine, and an old flask that has not even new wine in it." You never know who in the room may uncork a world of possibilities for you.

Rabbi Nachman of Bratslav attests, "The world is a narrow bridge. The key to crossing it is not to be afraid." How do we traverse that passage? With our second A: Ask a Great Question.

ASK A GREAT QUESTION

Which question? Any open-ended question that builds rapport. According to Proverbs, "Entrances are wide, exits are narrow"—your entry into the inner world of the people with whom you are networking can be as wide open as your imagination, but you want to keep the questions relevant and respectful. "How did you decide that you wanted to work in law/Jewish communal service/competitive eating?" is a better entry than "Do you like being a lawyer/Jewish communal service professional/competitive eater?" The first question gets you a story—a bridge to more conversation—while the second question gets you a nod (if you're lucky).

Author, speaker, and relationship-based marketing expert Larry Benet (who bills himself as the "Connector to Billionaires and Millionaires") offers some million-dollar (okay, billion-dollar) questions to get us in the networking frame of mind. These include:

- "How did you get started in _____ ?"
- "Where are you from originally?"
- "Where is your favorite place to vacation?"
- "Who is your favorite author?"
- "What's your number one personal goal for the year?"

These questions are engaging and, most important for the novice or nervous networker, simple! Asking an opening question isn't the time to show off how clever you are (as in "So, what do you think of string theory?"). It's the opportunity to get someone talking, and to get to know more about his or her interests—some of which you may share.

Here are some other conversation starters:

- "What do you do for fun?"

- "What has surprised you about your job?"

- "Who are some of your mentors?"

- "What's a typical day like for you at your job?"

- "What do you want to be when you 'grow up'?" (and say it with a smile)

And here's a win-win for both of you:

- "Where else do you go to network?"

ACTION PLANNER: ASK A GREAT QUESTION

Your turn! What questions have people asked you that really opened up a conversation?

1. _____

2. _____

3. _____

4. _____

5. _____

What questions might you try at your next networking opportunity?

1. _____

2. _____

3. _____

4. _____

5. _____

ADD VALUE

All of this leads us to the final A: Add Value. Too often, we think of networking as our chance to get something rather than give something. The book on Jewish ethics *Orchot Tzadikim* advises us that, "A truly generous person is one who always gives, whether it be much or little, before being asked." I must admit (with both true and false modesty) that I am memorable at networking events primarily for asking this question: "What kinds of connections would be helpful to you?" People are taken aback by my offer of help. They are surprised when I don't ask for anything in return. And most importantly, they are delighted when I follow up with what I've offered.

Networking is about two key elements: benefitting and contributing. While strategic networking can and should help you connect to people and opportunities that can propel you ahead in your personal and professional life, it also can and should help the people you touch along the way. Good networking is all about giving something of value and getting something of value. It won't be an even exchange, but it should be mutually beneficial.

Networking is about building relationships, and relationships are built over time. What do you know about the other person's interests or needs that will help you cultivate mutual interest? And why does that even matter? Imagine whispering into a cave—a whisper that you can hardly hear. Guess what? You will get a barely audible whisper in return. Now imagine yelling into a cave, "Networking stinks!" The cave will echo that sentiment right back to you, with the same words, tone, and volume. Finally, imagine saying, "I want to help you!" firmly and loudly into that same cave. What do you think you'll hear back?

It's the echo effect that allows us to hear our own messages replayed when we shout into a space where sound waves can bounce back to us. It's also the echo effect that allows us to see our own generous good will bounce back to us. If you are looking to activate your network, give to the people in it.

ACTION PLANNER: ADD VALUE

Ask yourself these questions to activate a powerful, positive echo effect:

1. Who in my personal network could use my time, support, or attention?

_____

_____

_____

2. Who in my professional network could use my time, support, or attention?

_____

_____

_____

3. Whom will I call or e-mail in the next week? (Name them here and schedule it!)

_____

_____

_____

Whether or not you are a fund-raiser, there is a dynamic and effective technique for staying in touch with your contacts that can be learned from the world of fundraising: "moves management." Developed by master fund-raiser William Sturtevant, "moves management" is a relationship-building system that takes prospective donors along a series of "moves" to get them more involved in—and more likely to give to—a philanthropic organization.

You can use the following "moves" to get your contacts more connected to you—and you more connected to your contacts:

GET TOGETHER: Set up a schedule to meet your contacts face-to-face, or if necessary, over the phone. If possible, meet them in places of mutual interest.

REACH OUT BY MAIL: This includes both old-fashioned (postal) and new-fashioned (e-mail). Send your contacts articles of interest, birthday or holiday cards, or anything that demonstrates that you know what they care about and that you're thinking of them. Be careful not to overdo it—you don't want to bombard them with unwanted or unnecessary mail.

INVITE THEM TO JOIN YOU: Ask your contacts to come with you to an event of mutual interest. Whether it's a sporting event, a concert, or a professional conference, a personal invitation can make an enormous and memorable impact on your relationship.

VISIT THEIR NECK OF THE WOODS: Visit your contacts on their territory—someplace that's important or convenient for them. It will help you learn more about what they care about. Remember that reaching out to others should be meaningful and value-added. Make your communication as personalized as possible.

None of these will cost you much in time, money, or energy—and any one of these things can make someone else feel special while making you memorable at the same time. As the Tosefta, a compilation of the Jewish oral law, reminds us, "Small coins add up to large sums."

Don't wait for an emergency before you pull out your AAA card. You can be networking right now to get some career direction or inside connection, and you can even help someone else meet their personal and professional goals. You're in the driver's seat: put your foot on the gas!

(Want to add value now? Pass this book on to someone else!)

PART 4

Get a New Perspective

20

Two Jews, Three Opinions:
Embracing Multiple Perspectives

I REMEMBER EXACTLY where I was on January 28, 1986, when the space shuttle *Challenger* exploded seventy-three seconds after liftoff from the Kennedy Space Center in Florida. School was closed for parent-teacher conferences that day, but my class had been assigned to watch the launch on television for homework. I was sitting cross-legged on the living room floor, watching the shuttle climb higher and higher, and then...disaster. There was an explosion of smoke, the plume splitting into two, and then the trail of destruction lingering in the skies. My mind couldn't register what my eyes were taking in, and I knew that I wasn't alone in my confusion.

What I didn't know then that I do know now is that confusion was at the heart of what caused *Challenger* to explode midair. According to the *Report of the Presidential Commission on the Space Shuttle Challenger Accident,* on the night before the launch, a group of engineers and a group of project managers met by teleconference to discuss whether or not the launch should proceed. The engineers felt strongly that too much stress was being placed upon the O-ring seals in the solid-rocket-booster case joints, which could result in, according to the team's memo, "catastrophe of the highest order—loss of human life." The project managers, on the other hand, were reluctant to delay the launch for fear that it would negatively impact the shuttle program's reputation for dependable delivery. They cited the fact that, despite evidence that O-ring erosion might cause significant problems, ten shuttle missions with O-ring erosion had flown successfully over the past year. As the two teams argued repeatedly over whether or not to proceed, Jerry Mason, senior VP and general manager of Morton Thiokol, the company that manufactured the shuttle, turned to the vice president of engineering and told him, "Take off your engineering hat and put on your management hat."

The leadership was right to recognize and acknowledge that there were two different perspectives at odds with each other. Where they

Hindsight isn't as useful as foresight ultimately fell short was in thinking that there were only two perspectives—the engineering perspective and the management perspective—worth considering. By limiting the discussion to an either-or choice—science or business—seven astronauts lost their lives that day and America's faith in the safety of its space program was severely compromised.

In hindsight, it's easy to say that the key decision makers chose the wrong perspective "hat" to wear for that particular decision. But hindsight isn't as useful as foresight. For all of us who are challenged every day with solving problems (hopefully not life-and-death ones), we want to know ahead of time which way of looking at the challenge will get us closer to the right decision or best course of action. That, of course, assumes we recognize that for any issue we face, there isn't just one way of looking at it. As Maimonides writes in _The Guide for the Perplexed,_ "People like the opinions to which they have been accustomed from their youth; they defend them, and shun contrary views: and this is one of the things that prevents them from finding truth, for they cling to the opinions of habit."

In their book, _Bozo Sapiens,_ authors Michael Kaplan and Ellen Kaplan agree: "The reason we have different hats to think with is that no single viewpoint can take in all of a complex world….[Our] fundamental assumptions about the world depend on different experiences and expertise."

I would add geography to that list. During my first Shabbat in Beijing, I was startled when the prayer leader announced, "Please rise and face west." West? Not east? Well, when you face Jerusalem from the other side of the globe, you're looking west. I couldn't have anticipated a more literal shift in perspective than this one.

"What's another way of looking at this?" is a frequent question that I ask my coaching clients, whether they are launching a career change, seeking a life partner, or trying to manage up, down, or across the organization. The question often stops them in their tracks. While most of us recognize that there are, indeed, multiple perspectives on almost any issue or challenge, we most often associate other perspectives with other people. *Of course* you know that your mother has another perspective on how you should potty train your child. *Of course* you know that your husband has another perspective on what makes a romantic anniversary gift. *Of course* you know that your supervisor has another perspective on the value of work-life balance. But have you considered all the other perspectives through which you might view your *own* issues? (And if not, then I've just introduced you to a new perspective! Welcome!)

What follows my question (and their answer) is often a repeat of the same question, "And now, what's *another* way of looking at this?" I don't want my clients to be limited to black-or-white (engineering or management) perspectives; there's another other way to see the problem, issue, or decision. As Rabbi Shira Milgrom writes in *Four Centuries of Jewish Women's Spirituality* (edited by Ellen M. Umansky and Dianne Ashton): "If logic tells you that life is a meaningless accident, don't give up on life. Give up on logic." In other words, there's always another, better view out there—if you're willing to see it and try it.

My client Ava came to coaching after she had been laid off from her job of more than twenty years with a management consulting company. Her default perspective was, "This isn't fair." After some discussion, it was clear to her that while she had every right to wear the hat of injustice, this perspective wasn't moving her forward—it was keeping her stuck. So I asked Ava to consider, in addition to it being unfair, what else was also true about her situation. She listed: "insulting," "unexpected," "challenging," "a change," and "an oppor-

Ask yourself, what's another way of looking at this? tunity." After reminding Ava that all of these perspectives could coexist—and that she didn't have to give up any of them—I asked her to pick which perspective would get her closer to her goals. Ava decided that "an opportunity" was the perspective that would serve her best. Our coaching work together focused on what she would do next now that she saw her situation as an opportunity. What Ava did was start her own management consulting practice, which is now thriving under her leadership.

With another client, Peter, we looked at whose perspective was most valuable. Peter was changing jobs within the federal government and was worried about how his contemplative, methodical work style would be perceived in his new position. His default perspective was that his pace was "too slow for today's busy workplace." I asked Peter to clarify whose perspective that was, and he was quick to identify that it was his former boss's perspective.

"How is his perspective going to serve you in your new job?" I asked him.

"I'm not sure. But I can't imagine that it will do anything other than interfere with my confidence."

"Is that what you want?"

"Not at all!" Peter exclaimed. "That's one of the reasons why I left."

"Who else has a perspective on your work style that you'd like to consider?"

"Well, my teachers always told me I was too slow."

"And how did that perspective impact you?"

226

"It didn't speed me up, that's for sure. It just made me try to hide it. So that one won't work," Peter decided, coaching himself.

"So what else?"

"Well, my daughter, Rachel, is slow and methodical like I am," Peter said, with some pride in his voice.

"And what would you tell her if her teachers were giving her a hard time about it?"

"I would tell her that her pace is perfect for her. I would tell her not to feel pressured. I would tell her that she has a special gift that will allow her to pay attention to what other, faster people will miss."

"Wow! What a terrific and supportive dad you are!" I exclaimed. "So…Peter, if you were parenting yourself the way you parent Rachel, what would the 'father perspective' sound like?"

"I would tell myself that my pace is perfect for me, that I shouldn't feel pressured, and that what I bring is a special and unique skill set that should be valued." Peter breathed out slowly.

"How does that sit with you?"

"I love it," Peter said. "I need to love this about me the way I love this about Rachel, and I need to remind myself the way I would remind Rachel if she needed to hear it."

"So, the 'father perspective' is the one you'll bring with you to your new job?"

"Absolutely."

"And remember," I told Peter, "you think Rachel is amazing. So keep that in mind about yourself, too."

"I will," Peter agreed.

Managing multiple perspectives in your own head is one challenge. Managing multiple perspectives within a group, team, community, or family is another. In her book, *Fierce Conversations,* Susan Scott contends that everybody owns a piece of the truth and most of us find it easier to stick with the reality we've defined from our perspective.

For example, in my work with nonprofit organizations, I find that both professional staff and board members struggle with the "whose responsibility is this?" dilemma. Staff members get firmly entrenched in their view that their job is implementation and that the board

Most of us find it easier to stick with the reality we've defined

should stick solely to issues of governance and policy. Or, in other words, the board should back off and let the staff do its job. That's the staff perspective, and there's certainly truth in that: in general, the role of the board is not overseeing the day-to-day operation of the organization.

But wait—there's more reality ahead! From the board's perspective, according to a 1996 *Harvard Business Review* article, "The New Work of the Nonprofit Board," board members often have little training in governance issues; they want to do more high-level activities, provide more hands-on help. When board members take on implementation tasks—tasks that are the domain of the staff—conflict occurs. Both groups—the staff and the board—are committed to clinging to the truth (i.e., You're doing my job!) as defined from their perspectives. Who's right? Both. Most groups need to be reminded that multiple, competing realities exist simultaneously. As a workshop facilitator, I am often asked to help groups see where there is both distinction and overlap in their perspectives of the current situation, issue, or challenge, such as what customer service means, why someone should make a philanthropic gift, or even what "success" looks like.

One tool that I use frequently is an exercise called "Graphic Jam," which I learned firsthand from Sunni Brown, coauthor of *Gamestorming.* In Sunni's workshop, we were divided into groups of five and were given thirty seconds to privately draw whatever word Sunni shouted out. The word was *freedom.* I immediately had a picture in my head that represented my perspective of freedom and scrawled it to the best of my ability. When time was up, we were given permission to compare and contrast our perspectives on freedom within our little groups—and then pick the one that was unique.

The other members of my group had a shared perspective on freedom that looked a lot like an American flag. But when I heard *freedom,* I immediately thought about the day that my husband and I decided it was time to let our nanny go after five years of live-in child care. Immediately upon sending her off, Michael walked into the kitchen and unbuckled his jeans, which fell to the floor in a heap. As he stood there in his boxer shorts, he announced, "I have not been able to walk around in my own house in my underwear for five years. This is freedom!"

My picture of *freedom?* Michael standing in the kitchen with his pants around his ankles. Nobody else in my group—or in the entire room—had drawn that same picture. But my picture of freedom was as real and true to me as someone else's Stars and Stripes, or bald eagle, or dancing on the beach was to them. And, as we all know, freedom isn't an either/or—it's not pants on the ground or a flag. Both are true.

Elaine Partnow writes in *Breaking the Age Barrier,* "Just as having opposable thumbs differentiates us primates from all other species, enabling us to grasp and wield tools and other objects in our hands, having 'opposable minds,' if you will, enables Homo Sapiens, unlike our primate cousins, to develop logic, self-argument, inner opposition, so that we can grasp any situation and mold it into an agreeable and useful shape with our minds."

Your perspective on any situation can hold you back or get you closer to where you want to go. If we only consider the "opposable" perspectives—either/or, black/white, engineer/manager—deciding which path to take can feel like a trap. But when we open ourselves up to a universe of options, the sky is our limit.

ACTION PLANNER

Think about an issue, challenge, or opportunity you are facing right now. Use the space below to write it down—focusing on what you want. (For example, "I want a promotion," or "I want to get married.")

_____

_____

_____

_____

When you think about this issue, what is your default perspective? (For example, the issue may be, "I want a promotion," and your default perspective may be, "It's never going to happen at this company.")

_____

_____

_____

_____

How is your default perspective serving you?

_____

_____

_____

_____

How is your default perspective holding you back?

_____

_____

_____

_____

What's the opposite perspective of your default—the one that's 180° away? (For example, if your default perspective is, "I'm never going to get a promotion at this company," the opposite perspective could be, "I'm going to get a promotion here—and soon!")

_____

_____

_____

_____

Really try on that opposite perspective for a few minutes—as hard or ridiculous as that may seem. What thoughts, images, and feelings come to you as you imagine that perspective feeling true to you? Which feels better or worse, more or less true, or just different?

_____

_____

_____

_____

What other perspectives or truths are possible here? List as many as you can think of:

Perspective	When I try this on, what am I feeling/saying to myself?	How does it get me closer to my goal?	How does it keep me stuck or push me further from my goal?
Example: "Go with the flow."	Stop pushing so hard, good things will come to me in their own time, everything happens for a reason.	It relaxes me, which might make me a more valuable asset at work—and happier, too.	It doesn't.

Who else might have a perspective or truth worth trying on? You can think about real people in your life (such as a parent, child, sibling, friend, or mentor), historical or biblical figures (such as Golda Meir, David Ben-Gurion, Eleanor Roosevelt, Winston Churchill, Moses, Miriam, King David), public figures (such as Jack Welch, Oprah Winfrey, the president of the Unites States), or anyone else whose mind you'd like to borrow.

Person/Perspective	When I try this on, what am I feeling/ saying to myself?	How does it get me closer to my goal?	How does it keep me stuck or push me further from my goal?
Steve Jobs, "Never be satisfied!"	I want more—and I want more now. What do I need to do to create the future I want for myself? What's my vision? How can I make it even bigger and bolder?	Maybe I should look for another job—am I playing too small? Something to consider.	Feels frustrating since I'm already dissatisfied.

In reviewing the perspectives you've tried on, which ones are worth further exploration because they get you closer to your goal? And how do you do that? (Examples include: interviewing people, writing in a journal, drawing pictures that represent your multiple perspectives, trying each of them on for a day or a week)

_____

_____

_____

After you've experimented with or chosen a new perspective, what do you need to do to make your new truth a reality?

My new perspective is:	I need to start thinking/telling myself/ acting as if/ doing:	I need to stop thinking /telling myself/ acting as if/ doing:	I need to continue thinking/telling myself/ acting as if/ doing:

21

Beyond Shehecheyanu:

Innovative Firsts that Deserve to be Observed

IN HER HILARIOUS and heartwarming book, *Just Let Me Lie Down,* author Kristin van Ogtrop laments the many endings she never saw coming, including the last time her baby would use a pacifier and the last time her growing son would let her walk down the street holding her hand. Because she didn't know that the curtain was falling on the final performance of these "unmilestones," van Ogtrop writes, she didn't know to anticipate, celebrate, or even acknowledge them until it was too late. Wouldn't it be wonderful if we had a system to alert us that "This is it!" when something important is about to end?

Until our smartphones are smart enough to do that for us, many of us will have to settle for firsts, not lasts. Jewish tradition offers the Shehecheyanu blessing as a way to mark the first occurrence of something or something we are doing after a long break. The good news is that the Shehecheyanu grants us a liberal list—we can say it for the wearing of a new suit as well as for honoring the first night of Chanukah. The Shehecheyanu gives us a moment to delight in the newness of what we're engaging in. It makes us sit up, pay attention, and reflect on the first time.

On a recent trip with my twins to visit my parents in Florida, I found myself wondering, "Is it Shehecheyanu time?" over and over again. You see, Grandma Nancy and Grandpa Ron are masters at helping the kids find the wonder, excitement, and firsts in their every-day Florida life.

Armed with little more than her grandma's encouragement, eyes that are impervious to camouflage, and an old dishtowel, Sophie captured her very first lizard on the hibiscus outside the house.

Shehecheyanu?

She kept this pitiable reptile and the two that followed their unlucky friend into my mother's trifle dish, until a quick trip to PetSmart revealed that caring for this tropical trio in New York would cost more than our plane tickets home. It was Sophie's first education in the difficulties of housing wildlife in an inhospitable climate.

Shehecheyanu?

Jacob, meanwhile, was thrilled when his grandpa took him out for his first breakfast at South Florida's all-cereal restaurant. Jacob combined seven different sugar-coated, tooth-destroying, strictly forbidden cereal selections into a bowl the size of a kitchen sink (and topped it off with chocolate milk) and dug in with gusto and a huge grin.

Shehecheyanu?

The next morning, my mother pulled her ironing board out of the closet and set it up in the kitchen to press a pile of napkins. Over their plates of eggs, Jacob's and Sophie's eyes grew large as their face registered another first. "Grandma, what's that?"

My children had never seen an ironing board before. (Don't ask. You'll end up giving me the same dirty look that my mother did.)

I thought, Shehecheyanu?

Probably not.

Blessing or no blessing, we owe it to ourselves, our friends, and our loved ones to mark firsts big and small. Firsts represent a dream developing, a step in the right direction, a milestone accomplished. My coaching clients and I have developed myriad ways to honor their firsts, ranging from writing thank-you notes to everyone who was involved in making their first win happen, to treating themselves to a well-earned, well-oiled massage. While celebrating the accomplishment of a hard-won goal can be an important way to honor a significant completion, marking the starting line is a signal to yourself that you've begun something meaningful to you.

Imagine running a marathon: What if the entire crowd of cheering spectators was gathered at the 26.2 mile mark? It would make for a spectacular finish, but the starting line would be a lonely place. As Taoist philosopher Lao-tzu once said, *Mark the starting line as a signal that you've begun something meaningful* "The journey of a thousand miles begins with a single step." Whether your endeavor is a thousand miles, twenty-six, or just a few feet, that single step—the first one—can feel the most daunting.

Nina had been working in advertising for eight years and wanted a complete change of pace and place. What she had in mind was finding a job as a US Foreign Service officer. While she was excited about the idea of learning new languages, living abroad for the next twenty years, and engaging with high-profile people around the world, the eight-step application, testing, and placement process would be rigorous. How would she stay committed and motivated? By dividing up the process into concrete, manageable steps and celebrating the start of each step as its own first. Nina and her husband went out to dinner at their favorite Mexican restaurant after step one: choosing a career track. Fortified by margaritas and motivated to keep going, Nina found ways to celebrate her firsts all along the way—until her successful appointment as an officer. Jack Welch, former CEO of General Electric, writes in his book *Winning,* "Work is too much a part of life not to recognize moments of achievement. Grab as many as you can. Make a big deal out of them."

Then there are the firsts worthy of reverence and respect. The first time you ask for help when you are struggling to find hope. That could mean asking for a referral to a therapist when you've felt sadder for longer than you can remember. Or it could mean walking into a gym and finding a trainer to help you get back the body you once had—or maybe never had but have always wanted. Perhaps it's the first time that you've cut a tie to someone in your life who takes far more than he gives. Possibly it's the first time you've suffered a serious personal or professional setback and were willing to sit with the disappointment and fear, rather than eat, drink, or medicate it away. To each of these I say, Shehecheyanu! Why? Because each of these represents a first time that you took care of yourself in a life-changing way—and that's worthy of repeating, again and again.

Every month, every week, and even every day, we ignore firsts that are worthy of notice. Of course we notice the traditional ones, like new babies and *b'nei mitzvah*. But we need to take the time to mark the firsts that get swept aside in the tsunami of everyday living: the first step on a path to a new career, a new relationship, a new commitment to your emotional or physical health. Wouldn't it be nice to take a moment to mark how far you've come on your journey to wherever it is you're going?

So here's a first I am excited to mark. Michael and I plan to take Jacob and Sophie on their first trip to Israel before their *b'nei mitzvah*. I can already picture us standing at the Western Wall at sunset as we recite a Shehecheyanu. I know that God's countenance will shine upon us and that God couldn't care less that we are praying in wrinkled clothes. Because that close encounter with the ironing board was my first—and my last.

This list is a reminder to honor the firsts among your family, friends, colleagues, and community. And maybe even doing that is a first for you worth honoring.

ACTION PLANNER

Here are ten new firsts worthy of noticing, celebrating, and continuing:

1. The first time you leave your iPhone or BlackBerry at home when you go on vacation or even out for dinner.

2. The first time you fit into the pants that were too tight for you, after weeks or months of exercise and healthy eating.

3. The first time you meet with a therapist or coach after realizing that you could benefit from talking to a professional.

4. The first time you say "I'm sorry" first—at work and at home.

5. The first time you say "no" without feeling guilty.

6. The first time the person you supervise at work accomplishes a major goal.

7. The first time your child makes a gift to tzedakah (charity).

8. The first time you solicit a philanthropic gift for your organization.

9. The first time your spouse or partner remembers to do the thing that feels really important to you (like unloading the dishwasher or packing lunches for the next day).

10. The first time you entertain guests and truly enjoy yourself rather than thinking about cleaning up.

What firsts would you like to celebrate for yourself, your family, your work, or your community?

The first time that: **I'll mark it by:**

1. _____

2. _____

3. _____

4. _____

5. _____

6. _____

7. _____

8. _____

9. _____

10. _____

22

Finding the Ah in the Oy

"I'M GLAD I CAUGHT YOU. I wanted to tell you a story about your kids," began the then-principal of my twins' Solomon Schechter day school. And despite her casual tone, I suddenly stood erect, sucked in my stomach (as if that would help), and readied myself for "a little chat" at home.

"So, Jacob and Sophie were playing basketball at recess together," she began. "And at some point, Jacob decided to sit it out. As he told me, 'I have a SPLIT-ting headache'. He said it just like that."

(Dramatic. That's my boy.)

She continued, "Every few layups, Sophie would come over to Jacob."

(She probably wanted to show off how many points she was scoring. So competitive!)

"And at a certain point, Sophie stopped playing and sat down next to him."

(As in, "All the better to hear you, my dear," I thought, channeling the wolf from "Little Red Riding Hood.")

"That's when Sophie rested Jacob's head on her shoulder and starting gently rubbing his head."

(Uh... what?)

"And she stayed with him, doing that, until the end of recess."

(Who was she talking about? Can this be true?)

It can be true. It was true. And what struck me the most is how all of these facets of my children can be true at the same time—loyalty and competitiveness, compassion and derision, family commitment and fierce independence. While I often fall into the habit of seeing my kids' deficiencies (so I can fix them, of course), my children's school principal viewed them through a lens that focused on their assets.

This isn't just a parent trap. Chances are you've found yourself at the office desperately trying to avoid having to work on a project with Dogmatic Dave. You might have walked counterclockwise around the kiddush table to circumvent Sensitive Sarah. Perhaps you've been ignoring Bombastic Ben's repeated attempts to join your organization's board (especially if you couldn't readily assess his financial gifts). And if you're like most people, you'll find abundant support for your perspective.

But what does upholding the deficiency perspective cost us?

It costs us time: long-held, ingrained flaws are not likely to disappear quickly, and waiting for someone to change can take the rest of your life—and then some. It costs us energy: focusing on failings is draining for everyone—especially for those of us who like to "fix" people. It costs us trust: when was the last time you think someone felt closer to you because you pointed out what was wrong with him or her—even if, especially if—you did it for "their own good"? It costs us progress: according to noted organizational consultant Peter Block, author of *The Answer to How Is Yes,* the most effective way to gain leverage in our relationships is to focus on the gifts that each person brings—their personal and professional skills and attributes—and give them opportunities to shine through work or volunteer assignments, or extra activities that highlight their assets. Instead of "problematizing" people and work, we need to remind our peers, loved ones, and ourselves what each of us uniquely and positively contributes to work and life. Whether it's someone's energy, keen eye for details, or uncanny

Focus on the gifts that each person brings

ability to be fully present in the face of a million distractions, each person has a gift to give.

Focusing on what's good about people, teams, and organizations isn't just about making people feel valued. Learning from others is a critical strategy. In their book *Switch,* Chip Heath and Dan Heath recount the story of Jerry Sternin, who worked for Save the Children in 1990 and was charged with fighting malnutrition in Vietnam—in only six months. Sternin recognized that the problems such as ubiquitous poverty, dirty water, and poor sanitation were "TBU"—true but useless information. He quickly realized that focusing on what was broken wouldn't yield him the results he needed. He didn't have the luxury of untangling root causes. He would need to try a less traditional but more productive tactic: focusing on what was working. In other words, he went to look for the gifts—however small they might be.

Sternin set out to search the community for what the Heath brothers call the "bright spots—successful efforts worth emulating." By finding a small but significant population of families who had been subjected to the same conditions, such as poverty and limited access to clean water, but who had managed to raise healthy, robust children, Sternin was able to extract critical information. The "bright spot" parents engaged in three activities that differed from non-bright-spot families—and yielded a much better outcome: (1) they fed their children the same amount of food, but spread the food over four meals rather than two to aid digestion; (2) they took a more active role in feeding their children (even by hand, at times) to make sure that they got the nutrition they needed; and (3) they added small shellfish and sweet potato greens—which cost them nothing, as these were "castoffs" from fishing nets and actual potatoes—to their children's daily portions of rice, giving them added minerals, vitamins, fiber, and protein.

Sternin's commitment to focusing on what was working well allowed him to learn from the families who knew something that he didn't.

He then gave those families the opportunity to teach others through cooking classes. The answer was a homegrown solution. Within six months, research showed that 65 percent of the children from these communities were better nourished. Over the next several years, the educational model that the researchers had established based on "bright spots" had changed the lives of over 2.2 million Vietnamese people in 265 villages.

Every day in our personal and professional lives, we have the opportunity to concentrate on what's distasteful or difficult—or focus on what's working well, what we want more of. Do we focus on and expect the worst, or do we pay attention to and expect the best? Do we see the coal or the diamonds?

When I am asked to work with a team or organization on a strategic plan—or, frankly, anything that sounds like "solve our problem"—I usually approach the assignment with a conversation about bright spots. Whoever I am speaking to, the executive manager or human resources professional, is eager to recount the range of behaviors, attitudes, and conditions that are acting as barriers to success. So when I ask them pointedly, "Well, what *is* working?" it's suddenly as if I've proposed marriage on a blind date. They go from sharing to speechless—I've asked a question that doesn't belong, that they haven't considered, that they aren't prepared to answer. Nevertheless, when given the opening, the opportunity, or sometimes the order (yes, I can be pushy) to shift their focus, most people are able to come up with something—no matter how small—that's working. And then my job is to take that gift, that bright spot, that golden nugget, and start building up from there, rather than tearing down people and processes.

Of course, there's a method to this madness, and its name is "appreciative inquiry." Developed by David L. Cooperrider at the Weatherhead School of Management at Case Western Reserve University, appreciative inquiry upends the tradition of focusing on weaknesses by focusing people, teams, and organizations on their positive qualities and leveraging those qualities to grow the group.

One of the core principles of apprecia-tive inquiry is the "Principle of Simultaneity: *The very first question starts the change."* So while my frequent first question, "What *is*

He searched for "bright spots"— successful efforts worth emulating

working?" is sometimes met with stony silence, I am unnaturally but tenaciously patient in awaiting an answer. Is it because I need to know what's working in order for me to be of help? Not really. It's because I need the person who has identified the problem to start the change process from the inside by coming up with an answer—any answer—to that question.

At the Passover seder, we traditionally ask the Four Questions that help us delve into the story of the Exodus from Egypt. (The unof-ficial fifth question for this and every holiday is, "When do we eat?") While there are many possible first questions that can help us delve into the story of what's going on in our organizations, I usually choose one that makes this question different from all other questions. The goal is to keep them from fixating on the bitterness of organizational life and allow themselves to remember and to taste the sweetness that binds the institution together.

Some of these first questions include:

- What's working?

- What do you want more of?

- What's possible?

- What do you value the most?

Each of these questions shifts the natural focus from deficits to strengths—and gently prods the person answering to admit that there's a desired state that may not be as unattainable as it seems.

While the principal of our school was concentrating on children at their best (and thereby helping to cultivate exactly that), I have found that many of my professional clients who work or volunteer for private

Do you see the coal schools focus their time, attention, energy, and
or the diamonds? resources on helping families surmount the barrier of the cost of education. And indeed, they think about "the problem" in exactly those terms: "Surmounting the barrier of cost."

Do you see what I see? The focal point is on a problem, the identified issue is overcoming a barrier, and the strategy is about how to stop concentrating on something that they don't want people to concentrate on. With all of this focus on challenges and roadblocks, what do you think will grow in this garden? You got it: roadblocks rather than openings and weaknesses rather than strengths.

So the question that kept me up at night was: How could we turn barriers into bridges when it came to helping families shift their thinking about private school education? This perspective change was important to me as a consultant working with a private school, of course. But, it was equally as essential for me as a parent of two children in a Jewish day school to adopt a new way of thinking. I was tired—and I'm sure my children were tired, too—of my literally accounting for every Jewish educational moment. If Sophie didn't want to say Hamotzi (the blessing over the bread) at Shabbat dinner, I would remind her that we were paying for her to learn and use that skill. When Jacob spoke his Israeli-infused Hebrew to a friend of the family, I would joke that we paid a premium for him to sound like a native. It was the educational equivalent of telling someone how much our house, our car, or our vacation cost. It was impolite at best and inaccurate at most. And that wasn't what I wanted my family to remember about Jacob and Sophie's school years: the price tag.

I knew I wasn't alone. Parents, school administrators, and board members were all in this boat with me, and I had a unique opportunity to shift the wind in our sails together. At the North American Jewish Day School Conference, I facilitated a workshop that used the subject of day-school affordability for an appreciative inquiry approach. This session's objective was to help key stakeholders (present company included) and school leaders shift their focus from the barrier (cost) to the opportunity (value).

With this goal in mind, I shared the four Ds of Cooperrider's appreciative inquiry:

1. Discovery: Appreciating the best of what is

2. Dream: Imagining what could be

3. Design: Determining what should be

4. Destiny: Creating what will be

Think about traditional topics you may have encountered in a workshop: "Conflict Management" or "Dealing with Difficult Customers." What are you setting yourself up to grow here? You got it: more conflict, more difficult customers, and probably a headache. Affirmative topics turn the subject around 180°. Doesn't focusing on "Fostering Respectful Relationships" or "Delighting Our Customers" make you feel more positive, enthusiastic, and engaged?

Our topic was "Shifting the Conversation from Cost to Value of Jewish Day School Education." By naming what we wanted more of, we took the topic through the four Ds.

1. Discover: Appreciate the best of what is

Drawing on the Heath brothers' "bright spots," I asked participants to think about a time when they felt that day school education was truly valued, honored, supported, and appreciated. What were the conditions that contributed to this? What were they doing? What were others doing? The energy in the room was electric as small groups of professionals and lay leaders shared stories about times when they were at their best. I pressed participants to eliminate "buts" from their stories (as in "it was a great school-wide event, but only because…) and to support one another in keeping their stories focused on the positive, and the positive only.

When we debriefed the groups, they shared examples that included engaging in community-wide events, press coverage of a student's success, a holiday program for parents and grandparents, students winning awards, and graduates coming back to share how their day school education had prepared them for their futures. While the answers were richly varied, the mood was universally uplifted. When I asked participants how they felt sharing their bright spots, they reported feeling proud, happy, and like a part of something bigger than themselves. Then I asked them to raise their hands if they felt that way when they were talking about the "affordability issue"—and it was as if the air had been sucked out of the room. Not a single hand went up. Nevertheless, I knew that the participants would want a chance to name the problems associated with the affordability issue, which remains a genuine barrier for many families. They wanted to be able to complain—even constructively. I promised them that we would neither ignore nor gloss over the problems, but that we were going to take a surprising path to get there.

2. Dream: Imagine what could be

Theodor Herzl, the founder of political Zionism, said, "If you will it, it is no dream." But before we could "will" the shift in focus from cost to value, we had to dream it. The Heath brothers call this "creating the destination postcard"—a positive, compelling, and possible vision of what you want to see crafted from clear statements and powerful visual images. To that end, I asked participants to think about this: "If you had three wishes for how people would feel about Jewish day school education, what would they be?" All participants got three sticky notes to write down their dream statements then posted them on the wall. I categorized them as best I could in the five minutes that I had. Dreams included that day school education would be seen as "a given" rather than as an option; that it would be viewed as "highly valued"; and that it would be regarded as "competitive," "inclusive," "worth every penny," "the investment of a lifetime," and "cutting edge."

What did this process yield? Three things: first, it allowed the group to put concrete words to what they had been wanting in their heads and hearts. Second, it permitted people to see that they weren't alone in their yearnings—by putting the notes into categories, I showed participants that many others felt as they did, which is how you start to identify allies in the change process. And third, this list, viewed through another lens, was their catalog of complaints. These "dreams" allowed them to name and see what *Create a positive, compelling, and possible vision of what you want* we didn't have enough of (a reputation as cutting-edge or academically competitive, etc.) without my ever asking directly about weaknesses or threats. Several participants commented that they would use this "indirect complaining" technique with students, parents, faculty, staff, and volunteers in the future by asking them what they dreamed about rather than having them name their nightmares.

3. Design: Determine what should be

The next step required some time travel. I asked participants to imagine themselves five years in the future and that—mazel tov!— they had just won a prestigious award for Jewish day school recruitment. They were asked to consider how they had transformed their school, their community, and the world; what existed now (five years later) that didn't exist then (today); and what other institutions were looking to learn from them. I offered them some simple Mad Libs to help them picture what the future could look like, such as, "I want our school to be known for _____" or "I want our school to become_____."

This gave participants the chance to think about certain "design elements" that might need to change, such as structures, policies, technology, leadership, and brand—as well as what was working and should be continued. Of course, these thoughts would need to be taken back to their institutions and discussed there—with the caveat that they should generate buy-in and start small.

4. Destiny: Create what will be

I must admit, I saved the best (read: most fun) for last. I broke the participants into two groups, "Heaven" and "Hell." The Heaven group was asked, "Imagine you had no limitations of time or money to get people excited about day school education. What would you do?" The list included fully subsidized Israel trips; bringing in the world's leading consultants and educators on a regular basis for staff development; recruiting high-level faculty by offering perks such as free housing, gym memberships, and new cars; and conducting complete technological overhauls for the school—iPads for everyone! While the group had fun fantasizing, they knew these were just pipe dreams. I pointed out that the purpose of this list wasn't to make them wistful about what they *couldn't do,* but that it was to look for themes among the dreams. When charged with that assignment, the group identified travel to Israel, staff development, hiring and retaining exceptional staff, and improved technology as key themes. While the original list looked impossible, this list seemed practical, desirable, and doable— which motivated participants to start asking themselves, "Where do we start?" An action-focused question, indeed!

The second group, Hell, was asked to tap into their *yetzer hara* (evil inclination) and consider this challenge: "How could you guarantee that nobody will ever want to enroll in Jewish day school?" This list included defacing the schools, ignoring the need for ongoing staff development, using antiquated technology, and focusing primarily on cost. This group was certainly not asked to turn their list into action items—quite the contrary. The Hell group was asked to look at what items on this list of "sins" they might already be committing that could be driving people away, such as unkempt property, poorly trained teachers, and the biggest elephant in the room, focusing on cost over value. By looking at their institutions, communications, and organizational behaviors through this lens, this group was able to create a "Stop Doing Immediately" list that served as their call to action.

At the end of the session, participants were excited on three levels: First, they were energized by the new focus on what was possible rather than on what the problems were; second, they were eager to bring the appreciative inquiry methodology back to their classrooms and boardrooms to apply this process to a range of conversations; and third, they recognized, like my kids' principal did, that institutions and individuals have a full range of bright spots to draw upon— if you are ready, willing, and able to focus on them.

How about you? Whether you need a boost of self-assurance, want to bring more shalom to your home, motivate your team at work, or help your organization make the case for what's flourishing rather than what's flopping, keep this in mind: *Leviticus Rabbah* (commentaries on the book of Leviticus) says, "The Holy One created light out of darkness." And you can, too.

ACTION PLANNER

1. What do you want more of in your work and/or life?

_____

_____

_____

2. What's already working for you right now?

_____

_____

_____

3. What are you doing when you are at your best?

_____

_____

_____

4. What are your gifts and assets?

_____

_____

_____

5. What comes most easily to you?

_____

_____

6. What do you value above all else?

_____

_____

_____

7. What three wishes do you have for the future?

_____

_____

8. What can people or organizations learn from you?

_____

_____

_____

9. What feeds and energizes you?

_____

_____

_____

10. What gifts have you exiled that you'd like to welcome back?

_____

_____

_____

23

Goose Bumps on Your Soul

ON A FAMILY VACATION to San Francisco, our kids had one goal: to visit Alcatraz. They had been looking forward to visiting the infamous island prison ever since they had seen it featured on a children's show about haunted buildings. They wanted to walk its dank corridors, stand in its creepy solitary confinement units, and, if all worked out as they hoped, have a hair-raising close encounter with its undead former inmates.

They couldn't wait to be shaken up. Their goal was goose bumps.

As I witnessed my kids experience the attractions of this historic locale, it struck me that they approached Alcatraz in stark contrast to how most grown-ups I know approach life. While the two of them peered around the jail's cracked corners eagerly seeking whatever shock, surprise, or specter might appear, too many of us run from the unknown rather than toward it. We cower in the corners of our lives, watching giant opportunities and new challenges pass us by because we're too scared to come out and play a bigger game in work and life. Of course, while none of us wants to set ourselves up for certain failure, the fear of the unknown seems more daunting than the pursuit of a new opportunity. We'd rather maintain the status quo than chance a shake-up.

In 1926 Harvard physiologist Walter Cannon coined the term *homeostasis,* which describes the human drive to preserve a stable physiological state when faced with stress and strain, possibilities and problems, and even excitement and exhilaration. Cannon believed that we naturally aim to achieve constancy through innate stabilizing factors—by keeping our heart rates down and our breathing controlled. To this day, many scientists agree with this view.

But Peter Sterling, a neuroscientist at the University of Pennsylvania's Perelman School of Medicine, disagrees. He believes that allostasis—our ability to adopt varying states to accommodate changing physical, psychological, and environmental demands—is at the core of healthy living. In his article "Principles of Allostasis: Optimal Design, Predictive Regulation, Pathophysiology, and Rational Therapeutics," Sterling makes this bold assertion: "Constancy is *not* a fundamental condition for life." As a coach, parent, and human being, I couldn't agree more. Not only is constancy not a fundamental condition for life, I don't even think it's a desirable one.

Sterling goes on to cite evidence of life that thrives under variable conditions, such as certain cell temperatures that can fluctuate by over 100° Celcius in the desert. Who knew? Another neuroscientist, Kelly Lambert, cites evidence that perhaps more of us can relate to—if you're willing to admit that you and rats have a lot in common. In her book, *The Lab Rat Chronicles,* Lambert writes: "If you are running a marathon, you will not live through the experience if your cardiovascular system does not change in various phases of the run to accommodate changing cardiovascular demands." For those of us who prefer more sedentary pursuits, Lambert observes that our health depends upon our body's changing production of insulin to regulate body sugars upon eating dessert. And she cites the adaptive production of stress hormones that kick in when we see a child run into the street—the very hormones that give us the boost we need to recognize an emergency and react immediately.

As a social scientist (darn you, organic chemistry!), I can cite many of my coaching clients who have learned to survive and thrive in unstable conditions that range from the bumpy to the goose bumpy.

For the last decade, Evan had worked as a fund-raiser for several nonprofit organizations. In each job, he courted prospective donors, making sure they felt connected to the organization's mission, became involved, and, ultimately, made a significant commitment of time and money to support the organization. While he had some experience in direct solicitation, most of his work had been behind the scenes—supporting other professional and volunteer solicitors, planning events, implementing campaigns, and developing donor recognition strategies. This was where Evan was most comfortable; he preferred to design from behind rather than be in a visible position. However, when Evan came to me for coaching, he recognized that his organization was undergoing some major changes, and he felt that his job was at risk. In response to challenging economic times, the institution had brought in a consultant to take them through a re-branding, re-visioning, and restructuring process. Over the previous three months, dozens of Evan's colleagues had been laid off, many of whom were similar behind-the-scenes employees. Evan wasn't sure what to do to keep his job and wanted some guidance.

It turned out, however, that Evan needed less guidance about how not to lose his job and more clarification about what he truly wanted. I asked Evan in our phone session, "What do you like most about your job?" and he shared with me that he liked the people, the hours, and the mission of the organization. When I asked, "What about your job gets you excited?" there was silence. Nothing. For a long time. I asked him if he was still there (which he was) and whether he had heard the question. He replied, "I did hear the question. And I can't think of anything. While I like my job, it doesn't excite me." Rather than assume anything, I asked Evan whether feeling excited about work was important to him. If it was not, then we could go down a different path. But I had an inkling that the shake-up at work was revealing a potential opportunity for Evan to do some shaking up of his own. And Evan confirmed that yes, he wanted to feel excited about work. And that's where our work really began.

Of course, our own definition of excitement is likely to be different from others'. Kelly Lambert wrote that her research assistant finds

As a public speaker, I get goose bumps for a living

skydiving both exciting and stress reducing—a reaction that is 180° away from her own. So I asked Evan to describe how he experiences excitement, and he mentioned a racing heartbeat, feeling flushed, butterflies in his stomach, an eagerness to get moving—all classic signs of an adrenaline rush. (Another classic sign? Goose bumps!) I asked Evan to think about the last time he felt that at work—and it was when he was asked to do a face-to-face solicitation of a major donor, for a $250,000 gift.

"It was awesome!" Evan exclaimed, in a tone of voice I hadn't heard him use ever before. "Terrifying, but awesome." And then, even over the phone, I heard him smile. "I want that."

Evan and I spent some time discussing exactly what the "that" was: challenge, risk, the opportunity to grow and to try new things. And before I could even ask the question that was swirling in my head, Evan answered it: "I think I need a total change of scene." Within only three coaching conversations, Evan had shifted his priority from how to keep his job to how to find a new one, possibly in a brand-new industry. What was at the heart of his change of heart? He wanted goose bumps. The instability in his workplace was a catalyst for Evan to seek new adventure in his career.

Over the course of several months, Evan and I identified possible industries that would allow him to find new challenges and apply his transferable skills. Within six months, he had found work where he least expected it: in retail sales for a luxury leather-goods brand. Evan's exceptional skills working behind the scenes to attract and retain high-end donors were transferable to his new role in attracting and retaining high-end customers. But the goose bumps got activated when Evan took his position on the sales floor, connecting clients to products that excited them—and him.

I understand Evan quite well because I get goose bumps for a living. I have been a professional public speaker for more than twenty years, and every time I speak I think of Mark Twain's quotation: "There are two kind of speakers: those that are nervous and those that are liars." Every single time I give a presentation, I experience some degree of fear. What if I mess this up? What if they don't like me? Or the worst: What if they don't laugh at my jokes?

Jerry Seinfeld once quipped, "If fear of public speaking is the number one fear, and fear of death is the number two fear, doesn't that mean that people at a funeral would rather be the guy in the coffin than the person giving the eulogy?"

Happily, only one part of my job is about scaring myself. The other part is about scaring others. I'm like the anti-ghostbuster: I'm hired to help people explore their fear rather than zap it at the source. We distinguish between the real, useful, and beneficial fears that serve a positive purpose, and the ghost stories—the tales we've told ourselves over the years to scare ourselves into limiting our hopes and dreams. Of course, I don't encourage people to put their lives or livelihoods at peril, but I do champion my clients as they risk behaviors, activities, attitudes, and expectations that will take them someplace new.

Goose bumps are one of my qualitative evaluation tools: Does thinking about making this change (exploring a new career, committing to a romantic relationship, rewriting your organization's mission statement, soliciting a major philanthropic gift, or confronting a toxic coworker) make your heart pound? Make you queasy? Make you want to run away? Good. Let's get started.

ACTION PLANNER

What do you really, truly want in work or life that you don't have yet?

_____

_____

_____

_____

_____

What's important to you about having that?

_____

_____

_____

_____

What scares you the most about going for it—or even having it happen?

_____

_____

_____

_____

What excites you the most about it?

_____

_____

_____

_____

What's the best thing that could happen to you if you got it?

_____

_____

_____

_____

What's the best thing that could happen if you tried to achieve it and failed?

_____

_____

_____

_____

What "ghost stories" are you telling yourself to keep the old way of doing this alive?

_____

_____

_____

What feels too frightening to risk?

_____

_____

_____

_____

What feels too frightening not to risk?

_____

_____

_____

_____

Whom else do you want to be on board?

_____

_____

_____

_____

What's it going to take to get you moving?

_____

_____

_____

_____

24

Whose Burden Is Bigger?
When Size Shouldn't Matter

MORE THAN TEN YEARS AGO, I was the overwhelmed, fatigued, barely bathed mother of newborn twins. Getting out of bed was a daily challenge; staying awake past 6:00 p.m. was even harder. So it was a real treat when my friend Wendy and my first-cousin-by-marriage Amy came over for dinner and a night of girl talk.

"You must be exhausted," Wendy clucked with compassion.

"I'm fine," I lied.

"How are you getting through the days?" Amy asked, her voice filled with *rachmanos* (sympathy) for me.

"It's no problem."

"Ah, then the nights must be getting to you," Amy pressed.

"No, really, everything is great," I responded, fearing that my nose might start to grow at any second.

What was wrong with me? Why wouldn't I let my two closest companions in on my exhaustion, fears, and concerns that this might never get any easier?

Because each of them had a burden that was much bigger than mine.

Two years previously, Wendy had been diagnosed with a rare auto-immune disorder, Wegener's granulomatosis. This vibrant, vivacious young woman dealt daily with a wide range of painful and debilitating physical symptoms that would elude remission for years.

One year previously, Amy had been diagnosed with metastatic melanoma, an insidious form of skin cancer that would rob her of her fertility before taking her life at age twenty-nine.

In what world was I entitled to complain about the burden of babies that Amy would never have or the temporary fatigue that was a permanent part of Wendy's life?

In their world.

"You are entitled to your own pain," Amy assured me, after the truth serum otherwise known as "no sleep" had forced a confession from my lips. "My having cancer doesn't mean that you aren't suffering." And Wendy, as generous as Amy, agreed.

These two, strong twenty-somethings gave me the gift of allowing myself to feel sad, bad, or mad without comparing it to anyone else's lot in life. And now, over a decade later, I am still thankful for this perspective that I rely on in my own work and life—and eagerly share with my family and clients.

For many of us who pride ourselves on being glass-half-full people, our natural instinct is to look for the light in the darkness. When someone is suffering, we want to remind them of the joy in the world, the opportunity in the challenge, the hidden gift in the disappointment they are facing. But our "drill, baby, drill" approach to unearthing something good for them under their dark reality represents our own need to make things okay, denying them their right to feel what they feel.

What does this sound like in practice? It often begins with these two words, "At least…"

"At least you have a job" (said to the person who is miserable at work, all day, every day).

"At least you're with somebody" (said to the person who is in an unsatisfying or damaging relationship).

"At least it's not cancer" (said to the person who is facing a different frightening illness).

These "at least" responses reflect the *listener's* need to feel better, to change the mood, or to fast-track a perspective shift that may be premature or might never come. It steamrolls right over the need of the speaker to experi- ence his or her own sorrow, without being *You can lament your losses and still find your way out* rushed or judged. Dare I say that even the Midrash (biblical interpre- tations) judges our burdens: "Put all other sufferings on one side of the scale, and poverty on the other, and poverty would be heavier." In other words, "At least you're not poor..." is meager comfort offered to someone who might be rich in dollars but in need of love, health, companionship, or even sleep.

When I work with clients who have suffered a disappointment or setback, I often notice when they rush to self-soothe. "I realize that not getting that job isn't the end of the world," one might say with a stiff upper lip, or, "I know I'm better off alone than with someone who didn't really want to commit to me." My job (as cruel as it might seem) is to acknowledge their willingness to shift into a happier place—and then invite them back inside their pain for a while. Too many of us feel that we're not entitled to mourn when others have greater losses, or that if we do grieve, we'll never leave that dark place.

But you can be sad in the face of others' sorrow, and you can lament your losses and find your way out. You don't have to earn the right to do this—it's the privilege you get from being willing to live life in all of its agony—and glory.

Alan D. Wolfelt is the founder and director of the Center for Loss and Life Transition. He agrees that mourning losses is an inalienable right. In fact, he created the "Mourner's Bill of Rights," a list of rights that those who are suffering can use to empower themselves to heal and to ask for and accept the kind of support they need. The first right on his list is: "You have the right to experience your own unique grief." Dr. Wolfelt gives us permission to despair—or feel any other emotion—without judgment, comparison, or competition.

My client David felt that he needed permission to experience the loss of a romantic relationship as grief—even though the end of the

It's the privilege you get from being willing to live life in all of its agony— and glory

relationship was his own doing. David, thirty-two, was a high-energy, successful attorney, who seemed to have everything going for him. Smart and funny, making an excellent living, and surrounded by a devoted group of friends, David knew that a bright future, professionally and socially, lay ahead for him. Romantically, however, was a different story. David was so scared of letdown that he hadn't dated in years, alternating between the fear that he would never meet someone and the fear that he would meet someone he liked who wouldn't reciprocate.

When David came to me for coaching, he was torn. He knew that he wanted to find a mate but wasn't sure what to do differently. When I pointed out, gently, that he'd been doing nothing, David did admit (with a reluctant smile) that this was true. By our second month of coaching, David was willing to try something—anything—to get closer to his goal, even though he was still scared of being hurt.

As his coach—and as someone who had met her husband through the prehistoric practice of placing printed personal ads in the newspaper—I felt uniquely qualified to help David. Choosing Internet dating as his low-hanging fruit, David wrote a personal profile, chose a photo, and uploaded his information to three different sites. Within a week, David had some (figurative) bites from a number of women who met his criteria. Over the next three months, David dated more than he had in the previous decade. He was experiencing the full range of New York City's single women, and he was even enjoying the process.

But by month four, David reported that something didn't feel right. The few women he was interested in dating again weren't interested in him, and someone he couldn't bear to see again was pursuing him doggedly. One woman, in particular, who was great on paper (read: screen), with whom he had been flirting online for several weeks, was completely different when they finally met in person at a café on the Upper West Side. It seemed like his greatest fears were playing themselves out in reality. But just when it seemed as if there were no fish left in his sea, David found his *bashert*—the person he was meant to be with—Jane.

David and Jane met at a book party for a mutual friend and hit it off when they both ordered whiskey sours from the bartender—who had neither whiskey nor sour mix. As they discovered that they shared the same backup beverage (dry white wine), they also unearthed shared interests in backpacking and spicy food, and learned that they had grown up three blocks from each other on Manhattan's Upper East Side. But with David having attended public schools and Jane private academies, they hadn't run with the same crowds. All of that was about to change.

Over the next four months, David and Jane became inseparable. They shared weekday commutes to work, weeknight dinners, and weekend gatherings with one another's friends. They backpacked through the Canadian Rockies. David brought Jane home to his family for the holidays, where they welcomed her with open arms. Even David's father, who wasn't easily impressed, told David to "hang on to this one." David felt confident enough in this relationship that he decided to terminate coaching.

It seemed that everything was going in the right direction when, over curry and candlelight one night, Jane dropped a bombshell: She didn't want to have children. David, shocked that she felt this way and flabbergasted that they hadn't discussed this topic sooner, asked Jane if she meant that she didn't want to have children in the near future—or ever. The answer was the one that David didn't want to hear: Not ever. In a moment, David's dreams of settling down with Jane vanished. He wanted children. She didn't. And while Jane argued that this could be a workable situation, David knew in his heart of hearts that it wasn't. This was non-negotiable for him. David ended things that night, and the romantic pursuit that David had worked so hard to initiate and nurture was suddenly, sorrowfully, gone.

Meanwhile, back in my office, I knew nothing of this. Why? Because as devastated as David was, he didn't believe that he had the right to mourn a relationship that he himself had decided to end. He believed that his grief—which he helped create—was unworthy of indulging. It wasn't until three months later, when he called me for some career coaching, that I found out how things had ended with the two of them.

"David, I'm sorry to hear about this. I remember how close you two had become," I offered.

"It's okay." David said.

"What do you mean by 'it's okay'?" I pressed him a bit.

"I mean it's fine. I'm fine. I mean, I am the one that ended it, after all. I didn't get dumped. I did the dumping!"

"Yes, you did end it. You were the one who did the 'dumping.' David, I hear some assumptions in there. Can I explore these assumptions with you?" I asked David's permission. If he really didn't want to be having this conversation (he had called for career coaching, after all) I would honor that.

But David agreed. "Sure."

"It sounds like you are assuming that because you chose to end it, you don't have the right to feel however you're feeling about the loss of the relationship, and Jane."

"Okay..." David listened.

"And it also sounds like you're assuming that it's okay to feel bad if you got dumped, but if you're the "dumper," so to speak, you don't deserve to feel bad."

David was quiet and then said, "Maybe."

"Maybe what?"

"That might be right. I don't even know anymore."

"What don't you know anymore?"

"I don't even know how I feel, because I refuse to feel it. I know that sounds crazy." David laughed.

I didn't laugh. We were at a precipice. ***What does "falling*** "David, it doesn't sound crazy—it sounds ***apart" look like*** honest. You said that you don't know what ***to you?*** you're feeling because you refuse to feel it, right? David, if you gave yourself permission to really feel what you're feeling, what do you think would happen?"

"I would fall apart."

"What does 'falling apart' look like?" I asked.

"I would be crying. I would feel like banging my head against the wall. I would be a mess," David said.

"Yes. Yes, you might do all of those things," I acknowledged. "And then what?"

"What do you mean?" David asked, confused.

"I mean after you experienced your grief—and we are talking about grief here—then what?"

David thought about it for a minute. "I mean, I guess then I would have to start all over again. Ugh, that will stink!"

"Yup, it probably will stink. And you'll do it anyway, right? Because you still want to find someone?"

"Yeah. I guess I'll do it anyway."

"So, David, in order to get you from where you are now to the other side of it, what kind of permission do you need to give yourself?"

David sighed. "I need to give myself permission to feel like hell."

"Good. And can I add something to that?"

David laughed, "Really? Hell's not bad enough for you?"

This time I did laugh, "It's a request, really. I just want to request that you give yourself permission to feel like hell for as long as it takes—and not compare it to anyone else's hell. Will you do that?"

"Deal." David said.

And David did deal—he dealt with his pain and his disappointment. And he also dealt with the internal struggle of knowing that he had been a contributor to his own grief and that he still deserved to grieve anyway.

A Yiddish proverb reminds us, "God gives us burdens and also shoulders." We need not compare those burdens or those shoulders in order to heal. While I am lucky enough to smile and hug and thank my good friend Wendy regularly and in person for sharing her burdens and shoulders with me, I send my deepest gratitude to Amy—wherever she is—for her shoulders—knowing that she is burden-free.

ACTION PLANNER

Using the list below, rank the "burdens" from most deserving of grief (1) to least deserving (25). (This list is adapted from "The Social Readjustment Rating Scale," by Thomas H. Holmes and Richard H. Rahe, in *The Journal of Psychosomatic Research.*)

_____ Death of spouse

_____ Divorce

_____ Marital separation

_____ Jail term

_____ Death of close family member

_____ Personal injury or illness

_____ Fired at work

____ Retirement

____ Change in health of family member or friend

____ Pregnancy

____ New baby

____ Positive change in financial state

____ Negative change in financial state

____ Death of close friend

____ Family argument

____ Bankruptcy

____ Taking out a major loan

____ Son or daughter leaving home

____ Trouble with in-laws

____ Beginning or end of school/college

____ Moving

____ Difficulty with boss

____ Minor violations of the law

____ Holidays (hosting or attending)

____ Other

Reviewing your rankings above, what types of losses, setbacks, or transitions do you feel are "most deserving" of grieving? Why? What themes do you notice?

_____

_____

_____

What makes these more deserving than others?

_____

_____

_____

Reviewing your rankings above, what types of losses, setbacks, or transitions do you feel are "least deserving" of grieving? Why? What themes do you notice?

_____

_____

_____

_____

What makes these less deserving than others?

_____

_____

_____

What losses, setbacks, or transitions have you experienced in which you compared your pain to someone else's? What did that feel like?

_____

_____

_____

What losses, setbacks, or transitions have you experienced in which someone compared their pain to yours? What did that feel like?

_____

_____

_____

_____

What could you do to stop comparing your burdens to others'? What could you tell yourself?

_____

_____

_____

_____

When you hear someone comparing their burdens to yours, what could you say to them?

_____

_____

_____

_____

25

Remember to Take a "Mazel Tov Moment"

ONE OF MY favorite movies as a teenager was *The Other Side of the Mountain,* based on the nonfiction book *A Long Way Up* by Evans G. Valens. In this inspirational and heartbreaking story, Jill Kinmont, a championship skier, suffers a terrible skiing accident, leaving her a quadriplegic right before her nineteenth birthday. The movie follows her long road to emotional recovery, including her life-changing, long-distance romance with Dick "Mad Dog" Buek, himself an exceptional skier and stunt daredevil. Dick proposes marriage to Jill over the phone, and she promises to accept his proposal—but only if he does it in person. While flying his plane to ask Jill face-to-face, Dick crashes into Donner Lake in California. In the movie, Jill's voiceover explains how she came to terms with yet another tragic loss in her life: "I remember the words that Dick Buek said to me the last time I saw him: 'How lucky I am to have found someone and something that saying good-bye to is so damned awful.'"

Jill chose to see one of her darkest moments as a reminder that she had experienced great joy. Her worst of times reminded her of the best of times. She saw in her loss a gift—that she had experienced such love in the first place. I remember watching this part of the movie over and over again, weeping into my Kleenex, and wondering how anyone—especially someone who had experienced such a life of tragedy—could see a gift in such grief. Jill's perspective seemed to align perfectly with these words of Midrash (biblical interpretations):

"If you want life, expect pain."

Personally, I think I would have a hard time seeing the blessing in the burden of losing the love of my life. Professionally, I can't imagine suggesting to a client—or even a friend—that they see a glass half

Sometimes a challenge is born out of a dream achieved

full in a desert of deep personal loss and despair. Nevertheless, over the years, I have known or worked with a few folks who have been able to tap into this perspective quite easily—it's impressive to hear them describe the potential for refreshing lemonade they see in the sack of bitter lemons they've been left to hold.

It's clear to me that other clients need permission to experience the burden they're bearing, with all of its sadness and disappointment. But there's a third group: clients whose current struggles are not a result of loss or calamity but a direct outcome of their achieving a major life goal. They've done what they set out to do—like making a long-awaited career change, finally finding a life partner, or even reaching a goal weight after years of ups and downs—but find that their whole lives haven't magically become as perfect as they'd pictured. When these clients hit a roadblock on the path between their "dream come true" and "now what?" I remind them of their "mazel tov moment," the one that got them here in the first place.

Like what? Like who?

Like my client Marc, who came to coaching to start his own coaching business. After months of attending coaching school to get the coaching core competencies under his belt, Marc began working with a tough, no-nonsense mentor coach (yes, that's me) to help him set a vision: for the types of clients with whom he wanted to work, for how he would attract those clients, and for how he could best market his business—all while working a full-time job to maintain a steady income. On one call, Marc told me that he had gained several new clients who wanted to begin booking their coaching sessions with him—and that he didn't know when he would be able to make the time to make those calls and do his job and spend time with his family.

"Mazel tov!" I cheered Marc.

Marc was confused and irritated. "What do you mean?"

"I mean congratulations on the fact that you're having this struggle. Because this problem means that you officially have a coaching practice."

Marc thought about that for a moment, and I heard his irritation transform into understanding. "Huh, I guess it does. It really does."

"And we will figure out how to handle this challenge, I promise you that. But can we take a moment to celebrate this problem? The problem you now have because you did what you set out to do?"

Marc agreed that, yes, we could and should celebrate the fact that he was where he wanted to be—with all of its ups and downs. He even decided to take his family out to dinner that night to make his achievement more meaningful, more delicious.

That's not to say that the problem of how to manage all of the moving pieces in his work and life wasn't real, too. It certainly was. But it was a challenge born out of a dream achieved—something all of us need to remember when we set our goals and imagine that life will be perfect once we attain them. As Henry Kissinger once said, "Each success only buys an admission ticket to a more difficult problem."

My client Elizabeth had been dating for over twenty years when she finally met her *bashert,* Ed. They opted for a short engagement, and Elizabeth spent the four months she had given herself to plan her wedding running from vendor to vendor and from store to store. One day, after she had spent ten hours looking for special shoes to go with her short, funky, lavender wedding dress, she called me and yelled (to me, not at me): "This is crazy! How can I make a wedding in four months? What was I thinking?"

"Mazel tov!" I answered.

"Save it for the wedding. If there is a wedding," Elizabeth growled.

"No, I mean think about why you have this challenge."

"Because I have a wedding date that's too soon, and I have a dress that's too weird!"

"Yes," I acknowledged. "And also because you have found the man you're meant to be with—and you're getting to marry him."

Elizabeth, who was rarely at a loss for words, was quiet for so long that I asked if she was still on the phone. "Yes, I'm here. You're right. I forgot about why I am even in this 'spin' to begin with."

"What matters is that you're clear about what's at the root of all of this. What can you say to remind yourself when you start to spin?"

I heard Elizabeth breathe out slowly. "I will tell myself, 'I get to be with Ed for the rest of my life. That's permanent. Everything else is temporary insanity!'"

I laughed. "I love it—'temporary insanity!'"

For the first time in many weeks, Elizabeth laughed, too.

Let me be clear: The "mazel tov moment" conversation is not a denial of reality. The struggles, stresses, and strains associated with finally realizing a major goal are as taxing as those that come along with the pursuit of the goal itself. The "mazel tov moment" comes from saying "yes, and" rather than "but" in a given situation. It's about acknowledging the current pressure as real and resulting from something good.

Compare and contrast:

- Marc had launched his new coaching practice—but he was trying to balance multiple demands.

or

- Marc was trying to balance multiple demands—and he had launched his new coaching practice.

Which one makes you feel more excited for Marc and what he has achieved?

How about these?

- Elizabeth was getting married—but she was overwhelmed.

or

- Elizabeth was overwhelmed—and she was getting married.

Which one leans into the joy?

Holocaust survivor, author, and president of the Center for Partnership Studies, Riane Eisler, writes in her book *Sacred Pleasure:* "Changes in consciousness are a very strange thing. Suddenly we see what was there all the time. And we wonder how it could for so long have been invisible to us." While we are struggling with the stresses and strains that are the organic by-products of our accomplishments and achievements, the "mazel tov moments" are there all the time. It is up to us to move them from the invisible to the visible realm so that we can honor them, celebrate them, and yes, deal with them, too.

> **The mazel tov moment comes from saying "yes, and" rather than "but"**

Rabbi Abraham Joshua Heschel wrote in *Moral Grandeur and Spiritual Audacity,* "Remember that life is a celebration—or can be a celebration....One of the most important things is to teach [people] how to celebrate." Even when we feel overwhelmed or underprepared, we need to take a moment to celebrate what we've already accomplished that brought us to today's dilemma. Yes, there will be another battle tomorrow—and how lucky we are to have found someone or something in life that is worth fighting the good fight.

Mazel tov!

ACTION PLANNER

What challenges or struggles are you facing right now?

_____

_____

_____

_____

Which of these challenges come from your having achieved (or being in the process of achieving) something important to you?

_____

_____

_____

_____

Without denying the reality of your challenges, use the spaces below to write yourself a "mazel tov moment" reminder for each of your challenges above. (Example: "Mazel tov on the challenge of trying to find time to train for a 10K—it means you've met your fitness goal!")

_____

_____

_____

_____

_____

What will you do to celebrate the moment—and the challenge you face? (Example: I will treat myself to a new pair of sneakers—which will celebrate the goal and motivate me to find some time to use them!)

_____

_____

_____

_____

_____

Who in your life may need a "mazel tov moment" reminder from you? How can you offer it in a way that doesn't deny their struggle—but reminds them that they've accomplished something important?

_____

_____

_____

_____

_____

_____

Acknowledgments

While "Oy Vey!" isn't a strategy, it *is* the first phrase that came to mind when I pictured sending my publisher the seven-page list of everyone who had helped make this book happen. I thought it again as I imagined belatedly remembering someone I had left off the list. So my approach to these acknowledgments is to start with my regrets for not including everyone who has contributed to my life and my ongoing learning, and keep my appreciation short, sweet, and specifically book related.

To my team at Behrman House, especially David Behrman and Terry Kaye:
Thank you for taking a chance on this unknown author and for letting me know right from the beginning that you were every bit as excited about this project as I was. You told me that this would be both work and fun—and you were right. Your partnership, support, and creative guidance have been invaluable to me.

To my other publishers: I want to thank Gary Rosenblatt of the *New York Jewish Week* for giving me my "Success without the Tsuris" coaching column that served as the backbone (and quite a bit of the flesh) for this book. Having to meet a writing deadline every other week was great training for writing an entire book. I also want to thank *Choice: The Magazine of Professional Coaching* for providing me with a writing platform that reaches my professional coaching community. Finally, I want to acknowledge that the chapter, "Put Your Network to Work," is being reprinted with the kind authorization of the American Jewish Joint Distribution Committee and www.jewishprograms.org.

To my book coaches (both professional and volunteer), Amy Ruppert, Tracie Shroyer, and Wendy Shanker:

Amy, thank you for consistently coaching me past my comfort zones and for holding a vision of what was possible that was bigger than the one I held for myself. Tracie, I deeply appreciate all of your technical support, which was actually emotional support thinly disguised as "research projects." And Wendy, the tactical, practical, and passionate education you gave me on how to write a book (without losing your mind) was only one of many things I am eternally grateful for in a friendship that has spanned over twenty years. Thank you for your head and your heart.

To my clients:

There would be no book without you. Thank you for sharing your burdens and blessings with me, as well as teaching me several lifetimes' worth of lessons.

To my extended, blended family:

When you have as many parents, step-parents, parents-in-law, siblings (half, whole, step), aunts and uncles, and cousins as I do, it's impractical to list everyone whom I need to thank. So let me thank every member of my family—by blood and by marriage—who gave me permission to publish a personal story that included them. Your willingness to be an integral part of this book was your gift of trust to me—and I will keep that gift close to my heart.

I thank the parents that I acquired as an adult—Joan and Archie Riegel, Ron Feller, and Valerie Grayson—who have offered generous, consistent support for my work and life. I must make special mention of two people who have been with me from my first day on the planet: my father, Fred Grayson, and my mother, Nancy Feller. In addition to all of your practical advice on publishing and writing (red pen and all), Dad, I thank you for teaching me to read the dessert menu before ordering dinner. If that's not a life lesson, I don't know what is. Mom, thank you for your boundless energy and enthusiasm for everything I do. You are and have always been the captain of my cheerleading squad.

To Jacob, Sophie, and Michael:

Jacob, your love for life and your insatiable curiosity for "what if?" and "why not?" is a model for what great coaching is all about. It's no surprise that this book is filled with your questions. Your sheer excitement for this book being published kept me on deadline better than anything else I could have imagined. Thank you for being my coach—and my son.

Sophie, I wrote this book based on how you play basketball: you don't quit, you don't complain, you don't want the rules bent in your favor—you just do the hard work, hope for a little bit of luck, and play as a team. Thank you for being my coach—and my daughter.

Michael, if anyone laughs and learns from this book, they have you to thank for that. You have filled my life with such happiness and growth that I believe it shows on every page. I wrote this book so that my readers would feel the way you make me feel—supported and special. Thank you for being my coach—and my husband.

BIBLIOGRAPHY

Antler, Joyce. *The Journey Home: How Jewish Women Shaped Modern America*. New York: Schocken, 1998.

Basco, Monica Ramirez. *Never Good Enough: How to Use Perfectionism to Your Advantage without Letting It Ruin Your Life*. New York: Touchstone, 2000.

—— "The Perfect Trap." *Psychology Today* (blog), May 1, 1999. http://www.psychologytoday.com/articles/199905/the-perfect-trap.

Baumeister, Roy F., and John Tierney. *Willpower: Rediscovering the Greatest Human Strength*. New York: Penguin Press, 2011.

Block, Peter. *The Answer to How Is Yes: Acting on What Matters*. San Francisco: Berrett-Koehler Publishers, Inc., 2003.

Brafman, Ori, and Rom Brafman. *Click: The Forces Behind How We Fully Engage with People, Work, and Everything We Do*. New York: Crown Publishing Group, 2011.

Buckingham, Marcus. "What Great Managers Do." *Harvard Business Review*, March 1, 2005.

Cockerell, Lee. *Creating Magic: 10 Common Sense Leadership Strategies from a Life at Disney*. New York: Crown Publishing Group, 2008.

Cooperrider, David L., and Diana Whitney. *Appreciative Inquiry: A Positive Revolution in Change*. San Francisco: Berrett-Koehler Publishers, Inc., 2005.

Covey, Stephen R. *The 7 Habits of Highly Effective People*. New York: Free Press, 2004.

Denning, Stephen. *The Leader's Guide to Radical Management: Reinventing the Workplace for the 21st Century*. San Francisco: Jossey-Bass, 2010.

Dobson, Michael, and Deborah Singer Dobson. *Managing Up: 59 Ways to Build a Career-Advancing Relationship with Your Boss*. New York: AMACOM, 2000.

Drucker, Peter F. "Managing Oneself." *Harvard Business Review*, January 2005.

Feltman, Charles. *The Thin Book of Trust: An Essential Primer for Building Trust at Work*. Bend, OR: Thin Book Publishing, 2008.

Ferriss, Timothy. *The 4-Hour Workweek: Escape 9-5, Live Anywhere, and Join the New Rich.* New York: Crown Publishing Group, 2007.

Foster D. J., and M. A. Wilson. "Reverse Replay of Behavioural Sequences in Hippocampal Place Cells During the Awake State." *Nature.* Advance online publication. 10.1038/04587 (2006).

Friedan, Betty. *The Feminine Mystique.* New York: W.W. Norton & Company, Inc., 1997.

Fusaro, Kimberly. "How to Be a Good Houseguest." *Women's Day.* http://www.womansday.com/life/etiquette-manners/how-to-be-a-good-houseguest-79800.

Glatt, Tom. "The Importance of Core Values." August 27, 2010. http://glattconsulting.com/2010/08/27/the-importance-of-core-values/.

Goldsmith, Marshall. *What Got You Here Won't Get You There: How Successful People Become Even More Successful.* New York: Hyperion, 2007.

Gray, Dave, Sunni Brown, and James Macanufo. *Gamestorming: A Playbook for Innovators, Rulebreakers, and Changemakers.* Sebastopol, CA: O'Reilly Media, Inc., 2010.

Heath, Chip, and Dan Heath. *Switch: How to Change Things When Change is Hard.* New York: Crown Publishing Group, 2010.

Heschel, Abraham Joshua. *Moral Grandeur and Spiritual Audacity: Essays.* New York: Farrar, Straus, and Giroux, 1997.

Himmelfarb, Gertrude. *The De-Moralization of Society: From Victorian Virtues to Modern Values.* New York: Vintage Books, 1996.

Holmes, T. H., and R. H. Rahe. "The Social Readjustment Rating Scale." *Journal of Psychosomatic Research,* 1967.

Iyengar, Sheena. *The Art of Choosing.* New York: Twelve, 2010.

Kaplan, Michael, and Ellen Kaplan. *Bozo Sapiens: Why to Err is Human.* New York: Bloomsbury Press, 2009.

Lambert, Kelly. *The Lab Rat Chronicles: A Neuroscientist Reveals Life Lessons from the Planet's Most Successful Mammals.* New York: Perigee Books, 2011.

Levy, Naomi. *To Begin Again: The Journey Toward Comfort, Strength, and Faith in Difficult Times.* New York: Ballantine Books, 1999.

Maimonides, Moses. *The Guide of the Perplexed.* Indianapolis: Hackett Publishing Company, 1995.

Martinuzzi, Bruna. *The Leader as a Mensch: Become the Kind of Person Others Want to Follow*. San Francisco: Six Seconds, 2009.

Maushart, Susan. *The Winter of Our Disconnect: How Three Totally Wired Teenagers (and a Mother Who Slept with Her iPhone) Pulled the Plug on Their Technology and Lived to Tell the Tale*. New York: Penguin Group, 2011.

Mayo Clinic Staff. "Job Satisfaction: How to Make Work More Rewarding." *Adult Health* (blog), Mayoclinic.com. http://www.mayoclinic.com/health/job-satisfaction/WL00051.

Morgan, Nick. *Give Your Speech, Change the World: How to Move Your Audience to Action*. Boston: Harvard Business Review Press, 2005.

NASA. *Report of the Presidential Commission on the Space Shuttle Challenger Accident (In compliance with Executive Order 12546 of February 3, 1986)*. http://www.challenger.org/about/assets/nasa_report.pdf

Partnow, Elaine. *Breaking the Age Barrier*. New York: Pinnacle Books, 1981.

Pink, Daniel H. *Drive: The Surprising Truth about What Motivates Us*. New York: Riverhead Books, 2011.

Pollan, Michael. "Out of the Kitchen, Onto the Couch." *New York Times Magazine*, July 29, 2009. http://www.nytimes.com/2009/08/02/magazine/02cooking-t.html?pagewanted=all.

Powell, John. *Why Am I Afraid to Tell You Who I Am? Insights into Personal Growth*. Chicago: Thomas More Association, 1990.

Pryce-Jones, Jessica. *Happiness at Work: Maximizing Your Psychological Capital for Success*. Hoboken, NJ: John Wiley & Sons, 2010.

Rao, Srikumar S. *Happiness at Work: Be Resilient, Motivated, and Successful—No Matter What*. New York: McGraw-Hill, 2010.

Ressler, Cali, and Jody Thompson. *Why Work Sucks and How to Fix It: The Results-Only Revolution*. New York: Penguin Group, 2010.

Rideout, Victoria, Donald F. Roberts, and Ulla G. Foehr. "Generation M: Media in the Lives of 8-18 Year-Olds." March, 2005. http://www.kff.org/entmedia/upload/Executive-Summary-Generation-M-Media-in-the-Lives-of-8-18-Year-olds.pdf

Rosen, Gerald M. *The Relaxation Book: An Illustrated Self-Help Program*. Englewood Cliffs, NJ: Prentice Hall Trade, 1977.

Scott, Susan. *Fierce Conversations: Achieving Success at Work and in Life, One Conversation at a Time*. New York: Penguin Group, 2002.

Sterling, Peter. "Principles of Allostasis: Optimal Design, Predictive Regulation, Pathophysiology, and Rational Therapeutics." In *Allostasis, Homeostasis, and the Costs of Physiological Adaptation,* edited by Jay Schulkin. New York: Cambridge University Press, 2004.

Taylor, Barbara E., Richard P. Chait, and Thomas P. Holland. "The New Work of the Nonprofit Board." *Harvard Business Review*, September 1996.

Terkel, Studs. *Working: People Talk about What They Do All Day and How They Feel about What They Do*. New York: Avon Books, 1975.

Tracy, Brian. *Eat That Frog! 21 Great Ways to Stop Procrastinating and Get More Done in Less Time*. San Francisco: Berrett-Koehler Publishers, Inc., 2007.

Tway, Dr. Duane C., Jr. "A Construct of Trust" (Dissertation, 1993).

Umansky, Ellen M., and Dianne Ashton, eds. *Four Centuries of Jewish Women's Spirituality: A Sourcebook*. Lebanon, NH: Brandeis University Press, 2008.

Van Ogtrop, Kristin. *Just Let Me Lie Down: Necessary Terms for the Half-Insane Working Mom*. New York: Little, Brown and Company, 2010.

Viorst, Judith. *Necessary Losses: The Loves, Illusions, Dependencies, and Impossible Expectations That All of Us Have to Give Up in Order to Grow*. New York: Free Press, 1986.

Walton, Sam. *Sam Walton: Made in America*. New York: Bantam Books, 1993.

Welch, Jack, and Suzy Welch. *Winning*. New York: HarperBusiness, 2005.

Wilson, Amy. "The Cost of Perfection." *Psychology Today*, January 1, 2000. http://www.psychologytoday.com/articles/200001/the-cost-perfection.

Wolfe, Ira S. "Trophy Kids: What Goes Around Comes Around!" *Business 2 Business*, March 2009.

Wolfelt, Alan D. "The Mourner's Bill of Rights." *Grief to Greatness*, 2007. http://grieftogreatness.com/professionalcommentaries.html#bill.

Wolfgang, Charles H. *Solving Discipline and Classroom Management Problems*. Hoboken, NJ: John Wiley & Sons, 2008.

Wright, Judith. *The Soft Addiction Solution: Break Free of the Seemingly Harmless Habits that Keep You from the Life You Want*. New York: Tarcher, 2006.